T0209140

HINGES

— DON POOLE —

WESTBOW
PRESS®
A DIVISION OF THOMAS NELSON
& ZONDERVAN

WestBow Press books may be ordered through booksellers or by contacting:

WestBow Press
A Division of Thomas Nelson & Zondervan
1663 Liberty Drive
Bloomington, IN 47403
www.westbowpress.com
1 (866) 928-1240

ISBN: 978-1-9736-9347-5 (sc)
ISBN: 978-1-9736-9346-8 (e)

Print information available on the last page.

WestBow Press rev. date: 6/12/2020

Revelations 3:20a - "Here I am! I stand at the door and knock." (NIV)

CONTENTS

INTRODUCTION

Pig iron. This is iron that has been refined from its ore and is in a crude form. Pig iron was named 'pig iron' because when they smelted[1] the ore they used sand channels to cool the smelted ore and those channels resembled a mother pig suckling her babies; pig iron. That is kind of what I am trying to do in these essays about the kernels of our faith that often get lumped into ores that haven't been completely smelted. These 'hinges' are the ingots of our faith that stand out as concepts we need to understand in order to understand the importance and relevance for our faith in Jesus the Christ.

What I am collecting in these essays is what I consider major 'hinges' in our thinking that we need to comprehend "how wide and long and high and deep is the love of Christ, and to know this love which surpasses knowledge -that you may be filled to the measure of all the fullness of God."[2] Did you notice St. Paul's use of 4 dimensions: width, length, height, and depth? Why the last one: depth? Some commentators on this verse see depth as an all-inclusive term that delves into the mysteries of God's love for us. As a science teacher I like to see the word depth as the fourth dimension: time. For all time God has shown love for us humans that we cannot comprehend.

What I am trying to do here is bring clarity to some this 'depth' that I have experienced in my walk with the Lord. I live in a house with 11 doors with 11 hinges. The larger your home, the more doors

---

[1] The process of heating an ore until it melts to get the base metal, such as iron. This has been going on for millennia.
[2] Ephesians 3: 18b – 19. NIV

on hinges you probably have. Each time you enter a room in your house, you change your perspective. Many times, I have walked into another room in my small house and forgot what I came in the room for. I learned not long ago, that when we go into another room in our home and forget what we came into that room for, we forget because our perspective has suddenly changed. We are in a different room with a different context than the one we just came out of, and that is why we 'forget' what we came into the room to get. The doorway is governed by a hinge. When we open the door to a different room, our perspective changes. That is why I call these essays 'hinges.'

You will notice that I write a lot about the cross of Jesus the Christ. And that is my intent. The cross is the central 'hinge' of our faith. The cross is the front door of our understanding of who Jesus the Christ was. In order to walk into the other rooms of our house of faith, you need to enter the front door. The cross provides the clarity for all the other 'hinges' of our faith. The cross opens the door to the resurrection that we like to focus on so much. The resurrection is the eschaton of our faith; a final point that we will all get to, thanks to the cross. As we open the doors to each of the rooms in our mental 'house of faith,' we need to view the whole context of **Jesus' life through the lens of the cross.**

I have to say a bit about my use of footnotes. I want you to focus not only on the content of my 'hinges' but on the footnotes, I use as I go along. <u>Please read them as you read my text. I guarantee they will help you understand my message more clearly.</u>

I need to explain a 'disclaimer' about my 'expertise' as an exegete[3] of the Bible. I am not an expert. I am not a theologian. I am explaining 'Scripture' as I see it, that has been explained and interpreted by me from the many books I have read and thought about. As of this year (2019) I have been a Christian or follower of Jesus for 50 years. This is my Jubilee Year. And God is not done with me yet. God is very patient and good. But as Peterson says in his book *Eat This Book:*

"Exegesis is nothing more than a careful and loving reading of

---

[3] an expounder or textual interpreter, especially of scripture.

the text in our mother tongue. Greek and Hebrew are well worth learning, but if you haven't had the privilege, settle for English. Once we learn to **love** this text and bring disciplined intelligence to it, we won't be far behind the very best Greek and Hebrew scholars. Appreciate the learned Scripture scholars, but **don't be intimidated by them.**[4] I have put in bold type what I consider the important points in this quote. I love the Bible; it gets me going. And I refuse to be intimidated by all the academia of the theologians who parse verse after verse of the Bible. They are very good exegetes, but so am I. That may sound arrogant to you, but I believe that God speaks to each one of us with the same truths that we discover in our lives of faith, only we see them in slightly different ways. We see them with differing perspectives, because our experiences in life are different.

And I need to make an apology. I am a teacher. I was a teacher for 28 years in public schools and taught adults for many years after that. I will explain definitions of different ideas and words as I write. It is just my style. Some people will appreciate this technique and others may not. Sorry. That is how I help make clarity in my writing. And you may disagree with my definitions. That is OK. There are many ways to see things. This book is about mine. My hope is that you will find some new ways to 'see' things as you read my book: *Hinges*.

This book is in three sections: The Sermon; In the World; and Not of The World. The reason for these three sections is first: The sermon on the mount is our constitution as a people of the Kingdom of God. Second: What is it that we are if we are 'In the World?' Third: What is it that the world around us **is** and we **are not**?

---

[4] E. Peterson; *Eat This Book;* Eerdmans Publishing Co.; 2006; p. 55.

FULCRUM

What is a fulcrum? This is a point about which a lever rotates. It is the hub of a wheel. It is your wrist when you are using a screwdriver. It is the hinge on a door. So, a fulcrum is important if you want to move something like a nailed board with a crowbar or a wheel or a door.

Archimedes[5] said: "Give me a lever long enough and a fulcrum on which to place it, and I shall move the world." A lever can move the world. Seems incredible that one man could use a lever and move the world. Yet, that is what has been done. And this fulcrum is the fulcrum of history. This is when the world moved. And here is the important thing to notice: the world was not paying attention to it. And also, it happened in places (fulcrums?) where not many people were noticing. It happened to Israel and it happened again in Jerusalem.

So, what in the world am I talking about? I am talking about the salvation of humans. The saving of us humans from ourselves and our preoccupation with ourselves. Salvation began in Israel when Abram (Abraham) was called to the other side to become the nation of Israel, but it got postponed until Moses led the people of Israel out of Egypt, across the Red Sea to the promised land that Abraham had journeyed through on his way to Harran[6]. And to this day that great event of salvation (Passover) is celebrated by our Jewish brothers and sisters.

[5] A leading mathematician, inventor, and philosopher of antiquity (Greek) 287-212 BC

[6] An ancient city in the region of upper Mesopotamia.

And then there is the second fulcrum of history that happened in Jerusalem: the crucifixion and resurrection of Jesus the Christ. From this event the Christian world and belief was formed with a mission to "make disciples of all nations baptizing them in the name of the Father and of the Son and of the Holy Spirit, and teaching them to obey everything I have commanded you."[7]

Us followers of Jesus believe that this second 'fulcrum of history' was the final statement to the world about the salvation of us humans here on planet earth. These fulcrums of history were the terms that "set the limits, established the boundaries, informed the conditions in which wars are fought, gardens planted, marriages arranged, goods and services bought and sold, elections conducted, funerals held, football games played, and meals cooked."[8] In other words, these two fulcrums of history were the real turning points for the world, not all the history that we learned in schools and universities about world history, or American history, or European history, or Asian history or African history. Believe it or not, those histories were the background for the real history- the salvation of us humans on this planet earth.

So, if that is true, why do we not learn history from this viewpoint? "Faced with the Divine, people took refuge in the banal, as though answering a cosmic multiple-choice question: If you saw a burning bush (Moses), would you- a) call 911, b) get the hot dogs, or c) recognize God? A vanishingly small number of people would recognize God."[9] Salvation is something that we cannot do for ourselves; it is God defined. God acts and we just stand still and wait for Him to do His/Her salvation plan. But that is not what us humans are all about. We want to do it for ourselves. We want to save ourselves and be in control of our lives. We want it all and we want it now.

History has taught us a basic assumption about the world that

---

[7] Matthew 28: 19a NIV

[8] E. Peterson; *Christ Plays in Ten Thousand Places;* Eerdmans Publishing Co.; 2005; p.178.

[9] M. D. Russell, *The Sparrow;* New York Ballantine, 1996; p. 100

is flawed. History has taught us that the world is at war and that it is normal to wage war. This teaching of history will not get us anywhere in achieving peace. And I don't mean peace as the absence of conflict. We need an alternate view of history that only God's salvation plan can give us. There have been many campaigns in this non-violent way of God's Kingdom inaugurated by Jesus the Christ. Sometimes these non-violent ways go unnoticed and relegated to the lesser parts of the teaching of history, but they were the more important strides that humans have made in order to eliminate the need for war.

For example; there was Mahatma Gandhi in India; there was Nelson Mandela in South Africa; there was Martin Luther King in America; the Peoples Power Revolution in the Philippines, just to name some. And they seem to be growing over time.

The example listed above are not the only events that we need to consider in how God's plan for salvation of humans on planet earth are affected. We are affected by the history that we learn in schools and colleges that has tainted our understanding of how once a government is in power it uses violence to maintain its power. "The democratic revolution brought the 'rights of man' and millions of willing recruits for war; the scientific revolution offered pure knowledge and better artillery and explosives; the industrial revolution created consumer goods and provided more material for larger and longer wars; imperial possession trade and spoils and strategic global position."[10] What Hauerwas is saying is that the revolutions that we learn about in colleges and schools brought with them the means by which a government can maintain its power through the use of violence that we call war. But we don't learn about this perspective of history, we learn about the battles and wars and machines of war that have made wars a way of life, even to the point of necessity in keeping the world 'free.'

Both Jews and Christians still celebrate these fulcrums of history, but more and more the world sees them as irrelevant or archaic, or

---

[10] S. Hauerwas; *War and the American Difference;* Baker Publishing Group; Grand Rapids Michigan; 2011; p. 49.

superstitions in a world that seems more and more governed by postmodern[11] thought. As our 'brave new world' plunges into the future, we have lost sight of the understanding that "he who is in you is greater than he who is in the world."[12]

Let me dissect this a bit more: Who is this "He" who is in me? In our 'modern' usage it would be "He/She." From what my grandchildren tell me I have to be even careful of my pronoun usage, as not to offend people of various gender orientations. Well, I am too old to worry about that. Anyway, the "He" in me is the Christ, Jesus. If you are not a believer in Jesus the Christ, then I cannot speak for who the "He" who is in you. Sometimes people get this reversed and the 'he' who is in the world is perceived as greater than the 'he' who is in me. *The Message* helps to clarify what this verse means: "My dear children, you come from God and belong to God. You have already won a big victory over those false teachers, for the Spirit in you is far stronger than anything in the world."[13] Notice this verse is based on an understanding that you know where you came from and who you belong to. A verse akin to this one is: "If God is for us, who can be against us?"[14] If we have the Spirit in us, then what is in us is stronger/greater than anything in the world around us. Now, if you don't know where you came from and who you belong to, then these verses become meaningless. Does everyone come from God? Does everyone belong to God? How you answer these questions is a hinge to your understanding of a belief in God. If you believe that God is the Creator of the universe, then you know where you came from. If you believe that we are all a product of chance, just one of the 'lucky' planets that life began on, then you don't know where you came from.

---

[11] A broad movement of the second half of the 20th century, encompassing a wide variety of approaches and disciplines, postmodernism is generally defined by an attitude of skepticism, irony, or rejection of the grand narratives and ideologies of modernism, often calling into question various assumptions of Enlightenment rationality.

[12] 1 John 4:4b, NIV

[13] 1 John 4: 4, *MSG*

[14] Romans 8: 31b, NIV I suggest you read verses 31-39 to get the full idea.

Of course, if you don't believe in God, then you don't know who you belong to. If you do believe in God, then you soon learn that you are His/Hers. If you believe in Jesus the Christ then you know that God is your father; Abba. So, you know Who you belong to.

So, it is paramount that we know Who is in us in order to rely on the strength of the Spirit within. This is a crucial understanding. All the events in our lives that threaten to destroy us and/or our faith in God are just that: events. They are not as strong as the Spirit that lives in us. The Spirit living in us will survive when all else fails. God has the final word in our lives, not the world about us. "The Spirit can make life. Sheer muscle and willpower don't make anything happen. Every word I've spoken to you is **life-making**. But some of you are resisting, refusing to have any part in this."[15] What Jesus is telling us here is that the only thing that can actually do anything in the universe is the Spirit. Where was this Spirit when the universe was formed?[16]

We live in a world that likes to think that everything in it started out physically.[17] What I mean by that is the only real things are physical things; atoms, molecules and ions. This is what we are taught – reality is made of 'things.' This is not the Biblical view. The Bible tells us that the physical world was made by Spirit- The Spirit of God. I might add; the **invisible** Spirit of God. You see, God is not the same as anything else. There is no substitute for God. He She is totally The Other. Incomprehensible. Indescribable. And it is from this Spiritual Being that the physical universe was made. Therefore, the Spirit is **life-making,** and life as we know it is a physical existence. In another sense you could say that the invisible made the visible and now it is our job as Christians to make the invisible visible. Confused? You are not alone. To me, this is a

---

[15] John 6: 63-64; *MSG*. I suggest you read the whole chapter to get the gist.

[16] Hint: Read Genesis 1:2.

[17] Science believes that the universe began as a 'quantum fluctuation.' This is a temporary change in the amount of energy at a point in space as explained by Heisenberg's uncertainty principle. Look it up for more information.

fulcrum point of our understanding; an orientation to who we are and **to** Whom we belong.

"Following Jesus accomplishes nothing on the world's agenda. Following Jesus takes us right out of this world's assumptions and goals to a place where a **lever can be inserted** that turns the world upside down and inside out. Following Jesus has everything to do with this world, but almost nothing in common with this world."[18] Here Peterson states my basic idea: The Christ event and the Abraham/Moses events are levers (and remember every lever must have a fulcrum) of history. The difference is that these fulcrums have everything to do with 'the world' but have almost 'nothing in common' with the world. This the very same reason that St. Paul in his letter to the Romans wrote: "Do not conform any longer to the pattern of this world but be transformed by the renewing of your mind." (Romans 12:2 NIV) And again in his first letter to the Corinthians: "For the wisdom of this world is foolishness in God's sight." (1 Corinthians 3:19 NIV) So, we are in this world, but have very little in common with it. But, in order to see this, we have to be transformed- our minds renewed; our vision cleared; our hearing tweaked. You will need a lever and a fulcrum to uproot your worldly ways.

---

[18] E. Peterson; *The Jesus Way;* Eerdmans Publishing Co.; 2007; p.270.

THE SERMON ON
THE MOUNT

THE SERMON[19]

Come on, Jesus, do you really think we can live in a world without lust, without hating our enemies, without seeking bad things for those who persecute and torment us? We have to resist evildoers, or they will kill us and take our possessions/resources. So, because we 'Christians' can't really believe that these commands in The Sermon are possible we need some form of our good friend 'rationalization' to help us out.

- These commands[20] of Jesus must not be meant for the political world of reality around us, but just govern our personal lives, so we make our salvation in Christ only personal and we don't talk about politics. (But then again, who is the law and Lord of reality? Hint: Jesus the Christ.)
- Maybe these commands of Jesus are just to help us feel guilty, so we can see how sinful we are and ask for more forgiveness.
- Maybe these commands of Jesus are just ideals we are to strive for, never believing we can ever achieve them in this lifetime.

---

[19] This is the Sermon on The Mount referred to in the book of Matthew; chapters 5-7. I call it The Sermon because of its importance to our faith as Followers of Jesus.

[20] I use the word 'command' here because these 'words' of Jesus that are often translated that way, are really commands, since Jesus is the Word (see John 1). Since He is the Word, his words are really commands just like the 10 commandments.

- Maybe these commands of Jesus are just Jesus' way of letting us know that we 'Christians' are a religion of forgiveness and not a religion of 'law' that is so aptly expressed in the Old Testament; Jesus is the fulfillment of the law and that means forgiveness.

- Or maybe we need some good reasons why Jesus died on the cross to help us feel 'at home' in the world, so we can be of the world and not just in the world. In other words, we need some ways of thinking to help us not get in the world's way, just to blend in and not be a 'bother' to the world. Maybe in this way we can teach the world to be more in line with Jesus' 'words' in The Sermon.

Our good friend rationalization helps us come up with what are known as 'atonement theories' about why Jesus had to die for us and our sins. This way we can separate the commands of Jesus in The Sermon from our personal salvation. The commands of Jesus are just his ethics, that don't affect our salvation.

See how easy that was? By using our good friend rationalization, we have separated the very one who is the law and reality into two parts: the ethics of Jesus (The Sermon) and the reality of Jesus (his crucifixion). How clever, but how cheap we have made the Kingdom of God.

Don't you see that you can't separate the ethics of Jesus and his crucifixion? They are both one reality. Jesus is constituting a people, a body politic[21] when he gave The Sermon. The commands of The Sermon are to help us depend on God and one another. We are to be a people who do not lust, curse, hate, brag, preen, worry, divorce, retaliate or backbite because that is what the Lord of law and reality commands us NOT to do. The Sermon is a description of the Jesus community gathered around Him. That is why the "beatitudes"[22] found at the beginning of The Sermon are like a key to The Sermon. These 'beatitudes' are who we will find among us in the Kingdom.

---

[21] Body politic – all the people in a single group.
[22] Matthew 5: 3-12 NIV

There will be those who mourn; there will be peacemakers; there will be poor in spirit; there will be meek; there will be pure in heart. Then the 'Church' can be the salt for the world and the light for the world. It is not a 'Church' that is hidden or blended into the world but a 'Church' that is on a hill, visible to the world, giving flavor to the world.

But what has the Church become? Since 325 AD or CE, we as a Church, have ever so slowly and subtly blended into the world around us, as we breath more and more of the air of atheism, and more and more become the allies of governments in the world, and at times we are almost indistinguishable from each other as the modern Church gives meaning and sanctity to the retributive violence of the governments of the world, placing them on equal footing with God by such phrases as "the divine rights of kings and queens;" "One nation under God;" "for God and country." Don't get me wrong. We are very fortunate to live in a nation with the best vision (so far) to begin a worldly vision that approaches the commands of Jesus in The Sermon. But America is a beginning at the values of The Sermon that Jesus inaugurated, and like all other beginnings in a government it is failing to uphold the basic tenets of its constitution, so well expressed in the preamble to The Constitution of The United States of America. And like all other governments before it, it will fail because all the governments teach us to depend on them and not on God. It's that simple.

We live in a culture where it is almost impossible to not worship money and our government. We print "In God We Trust" on the back of all our currency to remind us that we can have **both** God and money. We need to have the strongest economy, the strongest military, the strongest security as a nation, which makes us think we can't do without them or we will lose all we have accumulated in life. We won't get what we 'deserve' for all our hard work. So, in this environment of strength we lose our dependence on God. In fact, many people don't think we even need a God at all. If you call yourself a Christian, wealth is a big problem. Since we are the richest nation in the world with the highest standard of living, us followers of Jesus need to develop strategies that draw us away from the ways of greed that surround us every day. When we live in a nation where we think that our only means of security and strength lie in our possessions, then we live in scarcity fear! And our only chance of survival is to have more and more. Such thinking can only create injustice (i.e.: the rich get richer and the poor get poorer). Such thinking can only create violence (i.e.: protecting our interests in foreign lands).

But scarcity fear is not the way of the Kingdom of God. It is abundance not scarcity that rules in God's Kingdom. This idea simply overwhelms us. God's love, grace, inexhaustible creation, mercy and enduring purpose is all too much for us to understand. We are overwhelmed by a "tidal wave of glory."[23]

The Sermon gives us a way to discern those who are fellow travelers on this journey. What I mean by this statement is that we can tell (discern?) which members of our churches are the 'real' Christians and which ones are what I call 'cultural Christians.' For me, it means people who call themselves "Christian" but in reality, are really Americans first and "Christians" second. They make statements like "I am a Christian first and an American second," but then turn around and show that it is really the opposite by their actions. They cheer as American forces kill the foreign terrorists in other lands, or at home. They vote for people who will not defend the homeless, the lost or refugees from violence and war-torn countries. They cower in fear of foreigners and people that are different than them. These are the people I call 'cultural Christians.' They do not practice the commands of Jesus as clearly written out in The Sermon.

And here is where we run into one of the big problems Christians face: Do we want freedom or security? This is the question that each of us must answer in order to grow as a Christian or follower of Jesus. If we just want security then we will become cultural Christians, putting our country first and our God second. If we really want freedom, we will put God first and our country second. Our country touts the phrase "land of the free and home of the brave."[24] This is only true to a point, more accurate would be; 'land of the secure

---

[23] W. M. Cook; "The Tidal Wave of Glory;" 1876

[24] The Star-Spangled Banner: last line sung at ball games and other events.

and home of the brave.' We certainly have many brave warriors that protect and secure our land and our values, but at the price of our freedom. We talk about our freedom of the press and our freedom of speech and our freedom to assemble and our freedom of religion, but when these are practiced, our culture tries its very best to limit our freedoms of speech, religion, and press. Leaders advocate censorship and persecution of minority religions. They mock the press and divide our people into tribes. In other words, to me this means less freedom and more security. If everyone thinks and acts "American" as defined by our leaders, then we will be more secure, but not freer. Freedom lies in protecting the weak and differences among us, not the similarities. Freedom lies in treating each other as equals, not as inferiors and/or superiors. Freedom lies in humility not arrogance and pride. So then, answer the question: do you want to be free or secure? I think the cultural Christians have made their choice, what about you?

If you look carefully at The Sermon, that is what you will find; a lot of freedom to be and not a lot of security. Because when we actually practice the constitution of Jesus the Christ, we will be a people at odds with the culture of security around us. We will be giving away our resources rather than hoarding them. We will be loving our enemies, rather than trying to kill them. We will be praying for those who persecute us, rather than getting even. We will be at our best, rather than our worst. We will not be violent. We will be patient, kind, humble, seeing the best in others, enduring to the end. This is the people that Jesus constitutes in The Sermon. Are you one of them?

The Sermon is the source for many of the non-violent movements we have seen in the world in recent years (1900 to present day). If you trace the modern-day famous non-violent movements; Ghandi in India, Dr. Martin Luther King in America, and Nelson Mandela in South Africa you will discover that the roots of these movements were The Sermon that Jesus gave over 2000 years ago. Think about that. How long it has taken to even begin to develop strategies of non-violence?

"HOUSTON, WE HAVE A PROBLEM."[25]

This was a phrase that is now used to describe what happens when things go terribly wrong and we are trying to minimize the fear that is behind our statement. We try to stay as positive as possible so that our brain can work on the problem so that we don't let fear take us down the road to paralysis and total emotional breakdown- panic. And this is how we react when we encounter God.

All of us have encountered God, we just did not recognize it when it happened. I believe that usually it is a very brief and confusing moment in our lives that is easily overlooked and categorized as 'unusual,' so we store it in our brains as something that was due to some aberration in our daily routine. Many of the 'saints' in our Church have had these momentary encounters with God that they did recognize as God, and that moment changed their lives. This encounter we many times call a 'conversion' experience. If the experience happens in the right setting, or context, we have a pretty good idea that it was God. For example; many people have had an

---

[25] This was the often quoted, but erroneous phrase from the Apollo 13 astronauts when they encountered a big problem when they discovered that an explosion had crippled their spacecraft. This was the title of a movie made in 2016 about this mission. The correct quote was: "OK, Houston, we've had a problem here."

encounter with God at a revival meeting, or a church service when the pastor/priest gives what is known as an 'alter call.'[26]

The human mind is a wonderful organ and also a very willing participant in our need to be right. We love to find ways to support our need to be right, by rationalizing reality in any way we can. The need to be right is a very powerful need in our minds. To be right is to have control over something, to have something 'figured out.' This provides us with feelings of security and confidence in our abilities. And that is a problem for our ability to be humble. For it is really humility and not 'rightness' that is a hinge to life. We are more likely to be on the road to happiness if we are humble, then if we are always 'right.'

Our modern technology helps us in our quest for rightness. We can just 'look things up' on our smart phones. At our fingers is rightness. We can use it to show our friends their errors in thought or their lapses of memory. We can use our need to be right as we 'weaponize' our smart phones to do our bidding in our need for being 'right.' When we stay in our self-conceived world of being right, we begin to lose our ability to experience the supernatural that is around us every day. We lose our ability to experience the extra-ordinary that pops up when we least expect it. When we choose to be 'always right,' we choose to ignore the promptings of the Spirit to get our attention by the subtle changes that don't seem 'right' in our world.

So, with all this need to be right going on in the world: "Houston, we have a problem" becomes our mantra for keeping our 'cool' when things go terribly wrong and we can't seem to find the 'right' answer. Sometimes we reach out to trusted friends to help us in our dilemma of possibly being 'wrong.' Sometimes we reach out to therapists and specialists when we sense we don't have the 'right' answer. And if all else fails, we reach out to God, for an answer. And when this doesn't seem to work, we try to be 'right' in spite of the facts of our circumstances. "Don't confuse me with the facts, my mind is already made up!" Obstinance, our sea wall against 'wrongness.'

---

[26] This is a tradition in some denominations of Christians that usually takes place at the end of a service when people are asked to make a commitment to God and/or Christ, by coming forward to the front of the church.

I believe this 'need to be right' is so strong in our culture that we use our good friend rationalization all too often to 'prove' our point. Rationalization is quite different than reasoning. Reasoning, sometimes called just logic is one of the fundamental skills of effective/sensible thinking. But then we need to define what 'effective' and 'sensible' mean. Both of these terms circle back to 'reasoning' and 'practical' and the like. Again, using dictionary definitions doesn't seem to help in understanding the difference between 'reasoning' and 'rationalization.' However, the term 'rationalization' can point to a significant difference when defined- a way of describing, interpreting, or explaining something (such as bad behavior) *that makes it seem proper, more attractive, etc.* The part I have put in bold italicized type is what I want to emphasize. When we use rationalization, we search out a way to make our wrongness seem right. For example: Suppose you are deciding to vote for a particular politician. You like their ideas and you like how they handle themselves, but they say some really bad things about other people and have done some bad things in the past. How do you rationalize voting for this person? First you need to come up with an apriority. What is an 'apriority?' This is something that you believe to be a basic truth, or an assumption you make that is an over-riding principle of what you believe to be true. In my example above, it would be that I would vote for this politician because I like their ideas and the way they handle themselves and I would ignore the other traits because they are not part of my apriority. And this is an example of rationalization. And it is not reasoning. This is why I think being 'right' is so rampant in our culture today. We have a lot of people 'rationalizing' their behaviors, or choices in life rather than reasoning.

So, what is my point in being a follower of Jesus? You can't use rationalization when it comes to obeying Jesus. If you read The Sermon, you will find His commands for living in this world. They are very clear and consistent. As I have said before: We are to be a people who do not lust, curse, hate, brag, preen, worry, divorce, retaliate or backbite because that is what the Lord of law and reality commands us **not to do**. We can't rationalize these commands, even though the world around us does.

THE OVERPOWERING SENSE OF SELF

We are born into a world with an overwhelming sense of self. In fact, when we are born, we are all self. If you ask a two-year-old why the sun comes up, he/she will say something to the effect: "to warm me up." Everything in a two-year-old's universe is about them. Then we slowly learn there are other human beings in the world like us. We slowly learn there are other people with needs and wants just like us. We slowly realize we are not the center of the universe, even though some parents do their best to do otherwise, by indulging us, and prolonging the lies we tell ourselves about how important we are. Unfortunately, this can become a life-long endeavor of believing we are the center of the world around us.

If we grow emotionally, we learn about something called 'empathy,' where we can learn about the needs and wants of other people and begin to do things for these other people. We learn to give our money to a 'charity' or help people in need or buy people gifts that they want. However, many times this 'charity' toward others comes with a heavy price to our egos, so we want others to know how 'good' we are, how thoughtful we are, how generous we are. We want to be 'seen' for our gifts, our service, our 'good,' or our devotions.

And this is why Jesus warns us about our overpowering sense of self in the book of Matthew, chapter six: "do not let your left hand know what your right hand is doing,"[27] (in other words, be unaware).

---

[27] Matthew 6: 1-4; 5-8, 16-18. NIV

Or when you pray do it in secret (be hidden). Or when you go without things like food (fasting), do it so no one will know (again-hidden). So, Jesus is telling us to practice a kind of invisibility; a hiddenness to others when we do 'charitable' acts or show our devotion to God. So then, what does this hiddenness do for us? It disciplines us to become forgetful of ourselves. It helps us begin to lose that overpowering sense of self that we carry around with us all our lives.

But wait! How can we be the salt of the earth and the light for the world if we keep our 'good deeds' hidden? Our visibility, our saltiness is in following Jesus and keeping our eyes on Him. Our light to this world is our patience and suffering in a world that knows neither. So, when Jesus comes again and we are assembled before Him, "Then all the nations will be arranged before him and he will sort the people out, much as a shepherd sorts out the sheep and goats, putting sheep on his right and goats on his left. Then the king will say to those on his right, 'Enter, you who are blessed by my Father! Take what's coming to you in this kingdom. It's been ready for you since the world's foundation. And here's why: I was hungry and you fed me; I was thirsty and you gave me a drink; I was homeless and you gave me a room; I was shivering and you gave me clothes; I was sick and you stopped to visit; I was in prison and you came to me.' Then those sheep are going to say. 'Master what are you talking about? When did we ever see you hungry and feed you, thirsty and give you a drink? And when did we ever see you sick or in prison and come to you?"[28] And why were 'the sheep' unaware of these acts of devotion to Jesus? Because we 'sheep' have been cultivating a way to overcome our overpowering sense of self. And why did the 'goats' ask the same question? Because they never saw the needs of others in the first place. They were overpowered by their sense of self all their lives.

---

[28] See Matthew 25: 34-40; *MSG.*

REAL POVERTY

"When he came back to his disciples, he found them sound asleep. He said to Peter, "Can't you stick it out with me a single hour? Stay alert, be in prayer so you don't wander into temptation without even knowing you're in danger. There is a part of you that is eager, ready for anything in God. But there's another part that's lazy as an old dog sleeping by the fire.""[29]

This summarizes in a nutshell our real problem in this life. Unawareness. Being asleep, when we should be awake and alert. Sleepwalking through life, as danger lurks around us. Refusing to see the signs of evil having its way and we don't even notice. We are too busy. We are too involved in useless things, meaningless things that have no endurance or permanence in the universe.

What is the real, the rock of our life? What is the one thing we will remember when we are about to die? What is our real treasure? What is our real essence? These questions go unanswered. These questions are postponed for a later day. We are asleep. We are unaware. We are lost.

"The one difference between Christians and others is that we take God seriously and they do not."[30] And that is the real difference. Christians have a goal, and a means to get there. The world is all about accumulating possessions or wealth of some sort. The ends of the world do not have a goal, or a place to end up. The world ends up

---

[29] Matthew 26: 40-41; *MSG*.

[30] E. Peterson; *A Long Obedience in the Same Direction*; Intervarsity Press, 2000; p.108

in a nursing home with no purpose left to do. No work. No mission. Nothing but confusion and lies. Abandoned and alone.

"As long as it is day, I must do the work of Him who sent me."[31] In this verse Jesus is saying to us that we need to keep at work as long as the light is with us. Since Jesus is the Light, I would assume this to mean as long as He is in us: The Inner Man, Christ. Then, we are to continue working toward the goal, as long as we are alive.

I remember when I put my mother in a nursing home. She no longer seemed to recognize me; she just smiled at me without saying a word. It was kind of disturbing and unsettling to me. This woman was my mom, the person who I had relied on to love me and want the best for me. Where had this mom gone? The woman before me in the nursing home was just a shell. My mom was no longer there. Her work was done. Her awareness was gone. Where was my mom?

Before my mother became sick and needed to be in a nursing home, I remember a day when she was visiting me and my family. As she was leaving with my dad, she suddenly stopped and turned to me and said: "I won't see you again;" and she hugged me as if saying goodbye to me. I replied: "What are you talking about? I will see you next week." That was the last time I saw my mom for real. The next time I saw her, she had had a TIA[32] or two.

Even though I visited my mother's shell each week before she died, I knew that my mom had left and gone somewhere. My only explanation that I can think of was she was now with God and her Lord, Jesus. That is what I choose to believe, even today as I think upon this event in my life. I think that sometimes in this life our spirit leaves us and is remembered by our God, as He faithfully keeps our memories intact until the new creation.

My mom's death, both spiritual and physical is what I mean by the understanding of 'real poverty' and having the Light with us; the Inner Man. My mom's Light of life was gone and so was she; my real mom. And I knew the poverty of her absence.

---

[31] John 9: 4a NIV

[32] Transient Ischemic Attack. A brief episode of neurological dysfunction caused by a loss of blood flow in the brain. Another form of a stroke.

"The Spirit gives life; the flesh counts for nothing. The words I have spoken to you are spirit and they are life."[33] These words of Jesus are another 'hinge' in our thinking. "The Spirit gives life..." Note the capitalization. The Spirit being referred to here is God. The Holy Spirit. The Bible tells us two important things about God: "God is shear being itself – Spirit."[34] And: "God is love (agape)."[35] So, we have two clear statements about the nature of God: Spirit and love. Let me add another dimension (depth?) to this. God who is Spirit, created out of nothing which was Spirit. The universe was created from Spirit. Spirit gave birth to the universe. Then God's Spirit gave birth to a man we call Jesus the Christ: Spirit created again in the person Jesus, fully human and fully divine: Spirit. And what was Jesus' main idea that he taught in the Sermon on The Mount and when he was eating the Last Supper with his disciples? LOVE ONE ANOTHER, AS I HAVE LOVED YOU. Jesus the Christ was God's full explanation of love. The how and the why. And love was the axiom of Jesus: "**Love** the Lord your God with all your heart and with all your soul and with all your mind and with all your strength.' And the second is this: '**Love** your neighbor as yourself.' There are no commandments greater than these."[36]

---

[33] John 6: 63 NIV
[34] John 4: 24 *MSG*.
[35] 1 John 4: 16; center of the verse. NIV.
[36] Mark 12: 30-31. NIV

EATING THE ICING FIRST

When I was a kid, I learned to eat my cake first and save the icing on the cake for last, because that was the part of the cake that I enjoyed the most. I had learned to postpone reward, only I didn't know it at the time. According to modern child raising experts, one of the most important things you can teach your children is how to postpone reward. Back in 1972 a man named Michel did an experiment known as 'the marshmallow experiment.'[37] But it wasn't until many years later that the results of this experiment showed the very important idea of postponing reward, or delayed gratification. What they learned over 40 years of time, following the lives of these children from this 'marshmallow experiment' was basically that following the path of discipline (delaying gratification) over the easy path of distraction (eating the marshmallow right away) made a very big difference in the lives of these children (see the study cited below for details).

So, why do I bring this up in relation to a 'hinge' in our thinking as followers of Jesus? In order to explain this we need to understand the verse in Matthew chapter 6: "But seek first his kingdom and his righteousness, and **all these things will be given to you as well.**"[38] Peterson in *The Message* interprets this verse differently: "Steep your life in God-reality, God-initiative, God-provisions. Don't worry about missing out. **You'll find all your everyday human concerns**

---

[37] Jamesclear.com/delayed gratification. This is a good summary of Mischel's experiment and its findings.
[38] Matthew 6:33 NIV

will be met." I have highlighted the parts of the verse that are very similar. The important thing to see in this one verse is seeking/ steeping your life in God's reality- The Kingdom of God, and God's righteousness- God's initiative and provisions. All the other things that will be "given to you" or "your everyday human concerns will be met." These other things are the icing on the cake. The cake itself is God and his reality, righteousness, initiative and provisions.

With this idea in mind, consider what has been done to the gospel of Jesus the Christ. We have eaten the icing first and left the cake for last, if in fact we ever eat the cake. We have reversed our thinking about the gospel so that we can concentrate on all of our everyday human concerns and not the reality of God. So, what do I mean by that? What has become of central importance in the Christian Church today is the 'saving of souls.' We have concentrated on an idea of 'evangelism' to provide individuals with liberation from guilt, restored selfhood, self-discipline, moral behavior, and get us to our jobs on time and behaving well. And there is nothing wrong with that type of 'evangelism.' But that 'evangelism' is NOT the gospel of Jesus the Christ. That 'evangelism' is the icing on the cake, the **"all these things will be given to you as well."** Looking at 'evangelism' this way is like giving someone a Christmas bonus before he/she has done any work to earn it.

What does it mean to seek the Kingdom of God FIRST? What does it mean to be saturated in God-reality, God-initiative and God-provisions? For starter, it means that the Kingdom of God comes first in our lives and not our own personal salvation. We are Kingdom of God people, not people who are privately 'saved' for some Kingdom of God in the future. The Kingdom of God is NOW! It is a reality. Jesus didn't say the Kingdom of God is coming, he said "The Kingdom of God is near (or at hand, or come nigh)." Or in *The Message:* "The Kingdom of God is on your doorstep."[39] Or, more to the point when Jesus was 'pressed' by the Pharisees when the Kingdom of God would come, he told them that the Kingdom of God was "within you;" or in

---

[39] Luke 10: 11b NIV; and *MSG*.

The Message: "God's kingdom is right on your doorstep!."[40] So, it is clear that the Kingdom of God is a here and now Kingdom, the only problem is it doesn't look like any other kingdom. And as Jesus later said to Pilate: "My kingdom is not of this world."[41]

We are tempted to think that when Jesus said that His Kingdom was not of this world, that means that it is some sort of spiritual kingdom, that is invisible and, in the future, it will be realized. What I think Jesus meant is that you won't find His Kingdom among any kingdoms of this world. There is none like it. And there has not been anything like it, since Jesus said this to Pilate. We have tried many forms of 'kingdoms' from monarchies, oligarchies, dictatorships, republicanism, communism, totalitarianism, and of course democracies. Kingdom is a general term for some form of political government, particularly in the days when Jesus was on the earth. The closest type of government that we could say that Jesus was talking about was a theocracy, where God or gods are the ultimate source of decision making. But that isn't what I think the Kingdom of God is.

I think I need to use a metaphor to explain what I think this Kingdom of God is. Jesus used many metaphors to explain the Kingdom of God. (For examples, see particularly the book of Matthew chapter 13, where Jesus uses a series of metaphors about what the Kingdom is 'like.') My modern metaphor for the Kingdom of God is when we are all 'tuned in' to the same TV/radio station. In other words, we are all 'tuned in' to God. We are all listening and still; waiting on the Lord. And I believe it is when this happens that we will become the Kingdom of God, because we will have consensus and 'know' what to do next. Believe it or not, God CAN communicate with all of us at once. To me, that was the significance of what we call Pentecost: when the Spirit of God rushed into the world and people heard the message of God in all their differing languages; "because each one heard them speaking in their own language."[42]

---

[40] Luke 10:9 MSG
[41] John 18:36 NIV
[42] Acts 2: 6b NIV

THE CHURCH OF JESUS CHRIST IS A NEW LANGUAGE

If you call yourself a 'Christian,' you have a new language to learn to speak to the world. The world will not understand your language. You have a language of hope. The world will not understand you. The world around you sees your language as unreasonable because it is based on hope. You are not a liberal, or a conservative, or a humanist, or a whatever label the world wants to place on you. You have a new language of hope. Your language is revolutionary; it is not of this world.

"The business of the Church is to remember the future. Not merely to remember that there is to be a future, but mysteriously to make the future present"[43] We are a Church that makes the invisible visible. When we celebrate communion, we remember the future. Remember what Jesus says in Luke: "For I tell you I will not eat it (the Passover) again until it finds fulfillment in the kingdom of God. For I tell you I will not drink again of the fruit of the vine until the kingdom of God comes."[44] Jesus will eat and drink in the future when the Kingdom comes. So, in effect, we are making the future present when we celebrate communion. And that is mysterious. That is a mystery made known in the hiddenness of the present. It is another language to the world. It is the language of hope.

---

[43] H. McCabe; *God Matters;* Templegate; 1987; p. 141
[44] Luke 22: 16 & 18. NIV

"The WORD became flesh and made his dwelling among us."[45] In other words, Jesus, THE WORD became a human and lived with us: Emanuel -God with us. This Jesus was the language of God: THE WORD. The language that created the universe. The language that is Spirit and life. Without this language there is nothing. This is the language that answers the philosophical question: Why is there anything at all?

Language is what separates us from the rest of nature. Language is what we as humans have taken to higher levels in thought, symbols and signs. Language, in my way of thinking, was the forbidden fruit on the tree in the Garden of Eden, when we disobeyed God and ate of this fruit of language: knowing good and evil. Language is what the Tower of Babel was all about. Language was what the day of Pentecost was all about. And language is what separates us today. We speak differing languages; we speak differing jargons; we speak differing accents and dialects. These different languages separate us into groups with differing opinions and ways of thinking and doing. The world's languages keep us from unity.

When we meet someone, we determine what language they have. Where they come from. What accent they have. What words they use that give us a clue as to what they believe. What they say to us determines how self-centered they are or how caring they are. When I became a school teacher, I taught science. I had lunch with the other science teachers because they 'spoke my language,' they understood where I was coming from. We had a common frame of reference. English teachers ate with other English teachers; history teachers ate with other history teachers. We divided ourselves by what we taught our students, not knowing that we were creating differences among ourselves. We were separating ourselves by the jargons we spoke to each other.

Did you know that if we did not walk upright, we would not be able to communicate very well? Think about it. What if we had to walk on all fours, like our dogs and cats, would we be able to pronounce all the words that our soft lips require? We would have

---

[45] John 1:14. NIV

had to take in our food with our mouths, having hard tongues and lips, so that we would not injure ourselves every time we ate from the ground. That would limit our language considerably. By standing upright think of all the things you can do that animals can't do. Think about how we communicate, face to face, with our soft surfaces facing each other. Our vulnerable undersides available to the possible violence of another human. In nature animals go through all kinds of measures to protect their vulnerable undersides; camouflage, crouching, hiding, coloring, etc. Our very nature of walking upright is to help us communicate with each other.

It is our communication that is the basis of getting along together. "All of them were filled with the Holy Spirit and began to speak in other tongues (languages) as the Spirit enabled them."[46] Notice what gave the disciples of Jesus the ability to speak other languages (tongues): The Spirit. The same Spirit that created the universe. When we read this story of the day of Pentecost, we are tempted to think that the 'miracle' of everyone there hearing the words of the disciples of Jesus speaking in their native language was a 'miracle' because the disciples didn't know any other languages except their own. I think that misses the point of this 'miracle.' I think we need to change our thinking on this ability of the disciples to speak in other tongues/languages. What if it meant that the disciples had the patience and humility to hear the stories of the people who were present at Pentecost and that these 'foreigners' knew they were being heard from their own viewpoints and languages? How would that interpretation change the 'miracle' of Pentecost? What if what the 'foreigners' at Pentecost were hearing in their own languages was the language of God? How does that change your perspective of Pentecost? What if each 'foreigner' was really hearing the universal language of God, because that is the language of the Church of Jesus Christ?

"Now there were staying in Jerusalem God-fearing Jews from every nation under heaven."[47] Let's think about this verse for a

---

[46] Acts 2:4 NIV
[47] Acts 2:5 NIV

minute. These Jews came from all over the known world at the time. These were Jews, not Gentiles. And then after much explanation on who these Jews were at Pentecost, we learn that they were "amazed and perplexed,"[48] And we learn that some people there made "fun of them,"[49] accusing them of being drunk. And then St. Peter explains the situation to them. Now everyone at Pentecost is on the same page. Now they are ready to hear the gospel story in their own tongues/ language, and as a result 3000 were added to the Church of Jesus Christ that day.[50]

This way of 'seeing' the 'miracle' of Pentecost changes how I 'see' the language of the Church of Jesus the Christ. Our language is one of humility and willingness to hear the stories of 'foreigners,' so that they can hear the story of Jesus Christ. What is being experienced at Pentecost, in my opinion, is the experience of all of us being members of the family of God. There are no borders in God's family. There are no differing languages in the family of God. There are no liberals or conservatives in the family of God. We learn the dignity of differences when we speak the language of the Church of Jesus the Christ.

---

[48] Acts 2: 12a NIV
[49] Acts 2: 13a NIV
[50] See Acts 2:41 NIV. Read the whole chapter to get all the details of Pentecost.

A CULTURE OF LIES
AND VIOLENCE

You're not going to like this 'hinge.' We live in a culture of lies and violence. The lies take the form of propaganda. The violence takes the form of issues like 'gun control' and 'abortion' and 'global warming' and 'immigration' and 'nationalism,' or any other issue where there are people who are willing to kill other people who disagree with them, or who are 'different' than them. But the first thing you have to do to cause violence is lie. And the lies are found in their most common form: propaganda. One of the best definitions of propaganda is the spreading of ideas, information, or rumor for the purpose of helping or injuring an institution, a cause, or a person.[51] And those ideas, information, or rumor can be very close to what is 'true.' Because it only takes a slight twist of the 'truth' or omission of the 'truth' to get someone's propaganda across to people. And further we are subject to the lies of propaganda every day in the form of advertisements, opinions, and our rabid need for 'conspiracy theories' and strange happenings like 'ghosts' and 'yeti' and whatever 'monster' has been conjured up by some enterprising journalist.

So, this constant bombardment of propaganda can cause us not to even know that we are being lied to on a daily basis, since it is so common to our culture. So, over and over and over we see the evidence of these propaganda lies causing violence almost every day in our culture. We have mass shootings almost every week. We

---

[51] Merriam-Webster Dictionary.

have violent killings in each and every city in America. We have innocent 'bystanders' getting hurt and sometimes killed because of the carnage, caused by lies and ignorance.

But this violent way has been with us humans for a very, very long time. James and John (disciples) said to Jesus: "Lord, do you want us to call fire down from heaven to destroy them?"[52] But Jesus said NO! (He 'rebuked' them.) Yes, even the disciples of Jesus wanted to use violence because the people in Samaria (near Galilee) didn't welcome them. The spirit of violence was alive and well, even among the disciples of Jesus. When we think that God is on our side, we think that we can do anything to achieve His object-ives. Whatever it takes to bring victory to God! Let's look at history- There were the Crusades, The Inquisitions (Spanish, Roman and Portuguese for example), Cromwell's revolution in England, witch burnings in Salem, the conquistadors of South America. And I am sure you could come up with more examples.

I am often quite stunned (I guess that's the right word) by how 'getting even' by using violence as a means to do it, is ingrained in our culture. Rather than consistently in history, moving more and more away from doing things this way, we are moving more and more toward doing things this way. There seems to be little progress over the last two thousand years in becoming a less violent culture. My proof? Just read or watch the news each day.

We followers of Jesus are on a narrow road, and on both sides of us are two threats to our identity. The one on our left is the road of propaganda, and one on our right is the road of violence. Both trying to influence our way of doing things in the world. If we get distracted from the narrow way of Jesus, we will be 'of the world' and not just 'in the world.' It is only when we keep our eyes and ears focused on Jesus, the law and reality of life, that we can become the Kingdom of God.

"My sheep listen to my voice; I know them, and they follow me. I give them eternal life, and they shall never perish; no one can snatch them out of my hand. My Father, who has given them to me, is greater than all; no one can snatch them out of my Father's hand.

---

[52] Luke 9:54b. NIV

I and the Father are one."[53] And what happened right after Jesus said this? The Jews around him picked up stones to kill him! Violence-because those Jews thought they were preserving God's word as they perceived it, when the WORD was standing right there in front of them. And then, after Jesus tried to explain who he was to them again, he just "slipped through their fingers."[54] We are to follow closely to Jesus. He knows how to 'slip through the fingers' of violence. He is the Truth, the Way and the Life. There is no propaganda in Him. It is only on that narrow way that we can succeed as a Church and realize the Kingdom of God.

---

[53] John 10:27-30. NIV
[54] John 10:39 *MSG*.

THE COMMON GOOD

The 'common good' is that which is shared by and beneficial to all or most members of a given community. This is only one of two definitions given by philosophy of what 'the common good' is. The other one is pretty confusing. In other words, the 'common good' is what a community of people share as beneficial for their group. Let's put this another way: what behaviors and/or beliefs that we put into practice are those which will help us be in a loving/caring community of believers? And that, I think is a better way to see this idea called 'the common good.'

Well, before you go losing sleep over what this 'common good' is for us followers of Jesus, just go and read the Sermon on The Mount in the book of Matthew.[55] Here Jesus spells out for us what the 'common good' that we share and need to practice as Christians.

What individuals in a community or group share as their 'common good' can only be practiced if everyone in the group agrees on what those 'common goods' are. And that means that if we practice the 'common good' expressed in the Sermon on The Mount; we are a political group that shares the same language of the Kingdom of God. We Kingdom of God people speak the same political language. That doesn't mean we all speak English or French or Spanish. That means we all know what it means to not lie, or cheat, or steal, or preen, or lust or backbite, or curse, or hate, or brag, or worry, or divorce, or retaliate. (As I have written before.) How we behave is the language we speak as members of the Kingdom of God.

---

[55] Matthew, chapters 5-7 whatever version you like.

And most of that language is non-verbal. We don't need words to speak it; we need acts of love to speak in the Kingdom of God. We live in a culture that has a different idea of what the 'common good' is. We live in a culture that believes that the 'common good' is the sum of all the individual interests in this culture; this America. This culture believes that we are a mixture of 'common good' and that everyone's meaning of the this 'common good' provides this 'sum' of the culture's 'common good.' What a confusion this idea has created when we try to value everyone's 'common good' in the name of what we call politics in America. Every group has its own set of 'common goods' and every ethnic group is supposed to 'respect' every other ethnic group's 'common good.' What a mess. That is why we have so many problems with police officers, firefighters, and soldiers in terms of their 'authority' to do their jobs. And that is why our police officers, firefighters and soldiers bear so much of the cost of keeping law and order (social order). What if we had just one 'common good' and not a sum of 'common good?' What would that look like? That would be the Kingdom of God where God is the source of the 'common good.' And that is what the community of Jesus the Christ has to offer to the world.

TREES WALKING

"He (Jesus) took the blind man by the hand and led him outside the village (Bethsaida). When he had spit on the man's eyes and put his hands on him, Jesus asked, "Do you see anything?" He (the blind man) looked up and said, "I see people; they look like trees walking around." Once more Jesus put his hands on the man's eyes. Then his eyes were opened, **his sight was restored, and he saw everything clearly.** Jesus sent him home, saying, "Don't go into the village.""[56]

This healing of a blind man is only recorded in the gospel of Mark. This healing by Jesus of a blind man has been a curiosity to me for a very long time. This is the only healing that Jesus had to perform twice. Does that strike you as curious? It did me. I was fascinated that it took two tries for the blind man to get what we would call 'twenty-twenty vision.' The first attempt was obviously flawed, and the man saw "trees walking around." He had the proportions of people right but not the **clarity of vision**. And I think a lot of us have the same problem of the blind man in his 'seeing' clearly. We need some second healing or transformation in order to 'see' things are they really are. We need a new perspective.

We need Jesus to put his hands on our spiritual eyes, so that we can see clearly. We need not only a physical healing but a spiritual one as well. I think that is why this curious healing is in the book of Mark. "This, of course, calls for an energetic and lengthy campaign of conversation and perhaps better than conversation the **conversion of Christians** to the true anti-war dimension of their own faith

---

[56] Mark 8:22-26. NIV

and the **conversion** of all the enriching potential of their fellow humans."[57] What I want to point out from this quote by Stanley Hauerwas is the idea of a second conversion of "Christians." We are so ingrained with the ways of war and violence that we really need a second healing in our vision to get the perspective that we are not to practice war. "Ain't gonna study war no more," as the old spiritual song goes.[58]

So, how do we know that this 'conversion of Christians' is needed? First let me start with the Sermon on The Mount: "You have heard it said, 'love your neighbor and hate your enemy.' But I tell you: Love your enemies and pray for those persecute you."[59] Let's stop right here. How is war any way at all to love your enemies? War, simply put – massacre. They kill us and we kill them. Killing people is not love for people. So, when our real commander in chief (Jesus the Christ) tells us to "love our enemies," he certainly did not tell us to carry out 'just wars' in His Name. But, come on, war is necessary to protect ourselves from evil. Just look a WWII when Hitler and his Nazis had to be stopped. Certainly, that was a "just war" that needed to be fought. And this war may have been the closest that has ever come to the term "just war."[60] So, with this 'just WWII' in the past, a lot of questions need to be answered for the future, so that we can truly begin to study peace and not war no more. For example, questions like: What would a 'just war' Pentagon look like? What kind of military training is required that is willing to take casualties as well as victories in order to have a 'just war?' How would we elect

---

[57] S. Hauerwas; *War and the American Difference;* Baker Academic, Grand Rapids, Michigan; 2011; p.42. In this quote Hauerwas is calling for the abolishment of war.

[58] Ain't Gonna Study War no More" was originally a pre-Civil War spiritual that wasn't published until 1918 in a book of spiritual songs called *Plantation Melodies.*

[59] Matthew 5:43-44. NIV

[60] **Just war theory** is a doctrine, also referred to as a tradition, of military ethics studied by military leaders, theologians, ethicists and policy makers. The purpose of the doctrine is to ensure war is morally justifiable through a series of criteria, all of which must be met for a war to be considered just.

people with the patience necessary to ensure that a 'just war' would be the last resort to solving international conflicts? And these are just some questions that need to be answered before we have a 'just war.'

So, as a Christian, don't just take this "love your enemies" approach to life as unrealistic. That is the temptation. And the truth is in understanding that our enemies are our neighbors. They are the people that God puts in our path to love. They are the people that we have the most difficulty with, because they cause us harm and fear. It is much easier to put these enemies in a category of being less than human, so that we can destroy them. We are all (and I mean ALL humans) are made in the image of God. Not just the Americans; not just us Christians, but all humans are marked with the Imago Dei: the image of God. Let that 'fact' sink in. If you are a Christian or call yourself a follower of Jesus, you love anyone who is in your path during your days on earth. You spend your time, money, resources on the people who God puts in your path each and every day. This is the action of love. This is the 'second conversion' of your heart. So, stop seeing trees walking around and start to see people walking around.

OUR PLACE

We all come from a place. I come from Maryland. I come from Takoma Park, Maryland. That is the place I was brought up and went to school. That was the place that I put on my mail and packages that I sent to other people. They knew my place. We all have a place that we come from and either take pride in or not. For example, many Texans I know take pride in the fact that they come from Texas. Texans think big. There are a lot of jokes about Texans and the size of things. For example: when a Texan first saw Niagara Falls, he remarked: "We have a plumber in Texas that can fix that leak."

Each place we come from has a reputation of some sort, and many times a prejudice forms when we learn where someone 'comes from.' For example: when we hear a 'Southern accent,' what do we think about that person? Or when we meet someone from India or Iran, what do we think about that person? What prejudices do we have about the place a person comes from? It is important to recognize and understand our prejudices of 'place' if we are to become better at this Christianity that we profess.

Recently, a man who was originally from a foreign place testified in a court of inquiry about what he witnessed. Immediately the person he witnessed against accused him of being a traitor to our country, because he was an immigrant and said he had more loyalty to where he was from than the country he had immigrated to, even though he had served in our military and was wounded serving his adopted country of choice. This is how easily prejudice can form because of our 'place' of origin. This is how easily we can take on the role of bigot because of our pride of 'place.'

Where we come from as Christians is not our place. Our place is at the foot of the Cross of Jesus. This is where we belong as Christians. This place is Jesus. He is our place in the world. This is where a pathway between heaven and earth has been created by God. This is the place where love lives and where you came from does not count at all. This is a place where we are vulnerable and without protection. This is a place "where the desperate anxiety to please God means nothing; a place where the admission of failure is not the end but the beginning; a place from which no one is excluded in advance."[61]

At the foot of the Cross, history of the world and its struggles and competition have no meaning or logic. When we think that the meaning of history is to be found in the ordered structures of a given society, we begin to think that the history of God on planet earth is of lesser importance than the histories of the world that we were taught in school. We place God's activity in the world as lesser important than the histories of all the nations of the world. We become more 'worldly' and less Christian in our thinking. Think again what this verse in John says: "God so loved the world that He gave His only begotten Son.." To God the history of the world is about the salvation of the world. Not just one nation. Not just one type of people.

But beware of the steamroller of universality. What do I mean by that? We live in a culture that assumes that differences among us are a problem. If we all want to be Americans, we need to all have the sameness of the values of America. We all need to speak the same language. We all need to pledge our allegiance to the flag. We all need to sing the national anthem with pride. We all need to vote. We all need to fight for our country and die for our country if need be. And this is what I mean by the 'steamroller of universality.' Wasn't this country founded on the idea that "We hold these truths to be self-evident, that all men are created equal, that they are endowed by their creator with certain unalienable rights, that among these are life,

---

[61] S. Wells & S. Coakley; *Praying for England*; MPG books, Ltd, Cornwall; 2008; p. 175 (epilogue by R. Williams)

liberty and the pursuit of happiness?"[62] Tell me how the steamroller of universality accomplishes these 'rights?'

Are we not a nation of immigrants? Are we not a nation that comes from all over the globe? None of us are 'native' Americans. If we read our Bibles, we know we all come from Adam and Eve. They were the first spiritual humans. So, we all come from The Garden of Eden. That was our original place. And nobody knows where the Garden of Eden was. So, we don't actually come from any geographical place. So then, where is your 'place?'

---

[62] Declaration of Independence of The United States of America.

IN THE WORLD

GRACE NOT CONDEMNATION

As I read over the lives of some of the men who conceived many of the major denominations of today, I discover that these men, like Martin Luther and John Wesley had a period in their 'walks of faith' when they believed in a God of condemnation and not a God of grace. If you read their life stories, they went through periods in their lives where they preached a God of condemnation and not a God of grace. In fact, I believe that many theologians and 'believers' go through a time in their lives when they believe in a God of condemnation and sometimes even hate God because of it.

I have known this belief system in my life. I have known people who could not believe in a God who demanded perfection and needed to have his 'wrath' satisfied by the crucifixion of his Son. These people also refused to worship a God who wanted a 'fear of the Lord.' And I myself have been subject to this understanding of a God of condemnation. I think you could make a strong point in showing that the Old Testament of the Bible is in many ways a book that reveals a God who is strong on the condemnation points and weak on the grace points. And for that reason, many people erroneously believe that the 'God of the Old Testament' is a wrathful God that causes all kinds of problems for people who don't live up to His expectations.

In my way of thinking this grace/condemnation God is a hinge in the scriptures. We need to make a 'repentance' or turning point in our thinking and come to the realization that we worship a God of Grace and not a God of condemnation. The individual histories of men and women seems to hinge on this idea.

When we see only a God of condemnation in the scriptures, we have only seen the veil of simplicity and have not gone deep into the kernel of The Spirit that lies within the scriptures. Faith in God begins with the skeleton of the bare essentials of Truth and must lead us to the mature meat of the love of God for all men and women as Jesus demonstrates in His life and death as explained in The Sermon on The Mount.

In science as in religion there has been a debate going on for centuries about whether or not the universe or God can be 'reasoned' through linear logic or 'reasoned' through uncertainty thinking. So, what do I mean by that? Science illustrates this linear thought and uncertainty thinking in what is known as the Copenhagen Interpretation (uncertainty thinking) vs. the EPR experiments/paradox- which represents the linear thinking in quantum mechanics. Both 'schools' of scientific thinking are based on an assumption of believing in linear logic (reasoning) or non-linear logic (reasoning). In religion, theology has argued for centuries about whether God knowable or not, and 'if-then' statements regarding the relationship of God to His Son, Jesus. For example, some theologians through history, have concluded that God is unknowable and that His Son did not exist before God formed him from his Spirit at his birth in Bethlehem. This would be an example of linear thinking in theology. Other theologians have believed that God/Son were one through all time, as an example of uncertainty (non-linear) thinking.

Another way to express these two types of thinking (linear and non-linear) is a cartoon that I used to show my students: There was a chemist going through a series of steps to make a certain experimental substance. After each step he would exclaim: "Ah, just as I predicted!" And then he moves to the second step, making the same exclamation. At the final step of his chemical preparation the substance blows up. And there he sits with smoke coming out of his ears, his hair burned and his face blackened. I guess you have to see it to get the humor. Anyway, this demonstrates that linear thought can only get us so far. There is a lot of unpredictable things in the universe that we will not understand. This is certainly what happened when science discovered the quantum world. Very little linear thinking was required to understand the quantum world of sub-atomic particles, quarks, and relativity.

What is importance here is to realize that these two ways of thinking- linear and non-linear, have been with us for a long time. Many people want their thinking to be as certain and predictable as possible and they side with the linear thinkers. Some others want to believe that the universe and God will not be fully known, and they side with the non-linear thinkers. These people are what science would call 'uncertainty principle' people and the theologians would call them 'mystics.' So, I guess the important question for you to decide for yourself is which 'school' of thought are you in? Once you have decided that, you can read science and/or the Bible based on this assumption in thinking.

I think this linear/non-linear thinking is demonstrated in the four gospels: Matthew, Mark, Luke, and John. The first three are called the synoptic gospels. What means is that these three gospels include many of the same stories, often in similar sequence and in similar or sometimes identical wording. And they are chronological in their sequence- first this happened and then this happened. The gospel of John is not linear. In fact, John tells many stories about Jesus that are not in the same order as the synoptic gospels. John's gospel goes into considerable detail about what happened at the last supper; so, clearly John has a different thinking style and a different purpose in how he wrote his gospel. John's gospel is very conversational. The stories of Jesus that John relates are mainly conversations between Jesus and other people: Nicodemus, the woman at the well, the disciples, the blind man, Martha and Mary, the paralytic, the high priest, and Pilate. The book of John holds on to this conversational style. It is a very relational gospel. It is a very personal gospel. And I think a non-linear gospel.

You need to understand that the Bible is not a science book and should not be read as if it is. What I am suggesting here is that the thinking style we use as we approach the Bible and science is important to how we think about what the Bible or science means in our lives. Science has grown in importance in our modern world, as we use it to help us make good life decisions. The Bible has waned in importance in our modern world as we relegate it more and more to history and decide that it is not of much help in deciding how to live our modern lives. Yet, the Bible contains universal life lessons in how to live. The Bible contains solid, well thought out moral principles that we need to grasp if we are to live lives of meaning and purpose. So, this 'hinge' in your thinking style is of crucial importance. Do you believe in a God of Grace (non-linear thinking) or a God of condemnation (linear thinking)?

EXCLUSIVE/INCLUSIVE

A pastor once said to me: "The real problem facing the Church of Jesus the Christ is how inclusive we are." I think what he meant was how willing we were as a church to include all people in our worship and community. We have plenty of people in various denominations of Christianity who are all too willing to exclude people from their church. The exclusion takes the form of how they worship God, or whether they can take communion in their worship service or not, or if they are 'qualified' to teach Sunday school, or if they dress properly, or if they are hygienic or not, or if they are properly motivated to sing, or pray; and the list goes on.

And I believe it is this very notion of 'exclusivity' that has created the numerous denominations that we have in Christianity today.[63] What I notice as I read about the many denominations is that rather than an inclusive 'ity' at the end of the name they have an exclusive 'ism' at the end of the name of a denomination. What that says to me when we add the suffix 'ism' is that there is the formation of a set of unique beliefs to that sect or denomination that sets them apart from the other denominations. "I have given them the glory that you gave me, **that they may be one as we are one.** I in them and you in me. May they be brought to **complete unity** to let the world know that you sent me..."[64] What? Did the church not read this scripture? Did they just overlook it as not important? What were they thinking as

---

[63] The numbers range anywhere from 7 to 33,000 depending on how you define denomination and how you interpret history.

[64] John 17: 22-23a NIV (bold type mine)

they divided up into sects and denominations? I think I have a good answer: The need to be right. The need to have God figured out. The need to say we are right, and you are wrong. To sacrifice the unity of the Church of Jesus Christ on the altar of rightness, pride and yes, even ignorance.

"I appeal to you, brothers, in the name of our Lord Jesus Christ, that all of you agree with one another so that there may be **no divisions among you** and that you may be perfectly united in mind and thought… Is Christ divided?"[65] What? Did the Church of Jesus the Christ miss this scripture too? I think a I see a pattern here. I think what I see is that word 'sectarianism' rearing its ugly head. Whoa! What is this thing called 'sectarianism?' A good definition is: a form of prejudice, discrimination, or hatred arising from attaching relations of inferiority and superiority to differences between subdivisions within a group. In other words, when we see our beliefs and interpretations of the Church of Jesus Christ as superior to other members of our church or denomination. And then what do we do? We argue. We quarrel. And the next thing you know the group of people who feel the greatest need to be right form another sect, or in time another denomination. And off we go again dividing the body of Christ- again.

"Babel is the mother city of sectarianism."[66] Do you remember the story in Genesis about the tower of Babel?[67] What is often overlooked in this story is the reason the Lord confused the language of the city in the story. They were attempting to build a tower to "reach the heavens so that we may make a name for ourselves." (verse 4) They were attempting to remove God. They were going to be self-sufficient. They were going to do it all by themselves. They didn't need God. God was becoming less and less, and the people of the city were becoming more and more important. Sound familiar? It is.

And what goes unnoticed is how easily this self-sufficiency

---

[65] 1 Corinthians 1:10; 13a. NIV

[66] E. Peterson; *Christ Plays in Ten Thousand Places;* Eerdman's Publishing Co.; 2005; p.242.

[67] See Genesis 11: 1-9. NIV

gets planted in the Church of Jesus the Christ. It begins with the destructive form of pride called narcissism. A good definition of narcissism is: a grandiose view of oneself; have problems empathizing with other people; a sense of entitlement; a need for admiration and/ or attention. Also, narcissism is a spectrum. Only a small percentage of people (about 1%) are truly narcissists and only some of these narcissists become NPD (Narcissistic Personality Disorder). These narcissists are sometimes very charismatic people, with great self-confidence and wonderful speaking and writing skills. When these narcissists invade the Church of Jesus the Christ; we have a problem.

These narcissistic invaders are very good at propaganda and how to influence people and how they think. But, if you notice, their loyalties are not to God but to themselves. That is why St. Paul went on further to say: "Was Paul crucified for you? Were you baptized in the name of Paul?"[68] St. Paul was stressing that we are in the Church of Jesus the Christ, not the church of Paul of Tarsus; or the church of Pastor Mark, or Pastor Melissa. So then, when you go to a church because you agree with the pastor's philosophy or how good he or she does the sermons, or because you like the way they do 'church,' make sure that it matches God's way; the way of Jesus the Christ. The way of Jesus the Christ is very well summarized in The Sermon on The Mount in the book of Matthew. There is no exclusivity in this sermon. We are all included in the Kingdom of God. In God's Kingdom there are no Methodists, or Catholics, or Lutherans or Pentecostals, or whatever sect or denominations you like to belong to.

"In my Father's House are many rooms; if it were not so, I would have told you. I am going there to prepare a place for *you*."[69] Jesus is preparing a place for me, not my denomination or sect. "It's a big, big house with lots and lots of room; a big, big table with lots and lots of food… It's my Father's house."[70]

---

[68] 1 Corinthians 1:13b. NIV

[69] John 14: 2. NIV (emphasis mine)

[70] Lyrics from "Big House" by Audio Adrenaline; 1993 album "Don't Censor Me;" 1993.

KING NUMBER

Quantifying- the act of counting and measuring; gathering data. Can animals count? Yes, they can, but they don't all use the same part of the brain. Do they know numbers? Probably not, but they can tell larger and smaller quantities. But us humans are the only animals that have taken numbers and quantifying to higher and higher realms: algebra, geometry, calculus. Animals can't do those forms of quantifying.

So, what's the point. The point is that we have learned to take numbers seriously. In fact, for many people numbers are king. How much money do you make has become a ruler (measuring stick) for how successful you are, or how popular you are, or how smart you are: obviously people who make a lot of money are smart, aren't they? Or, how many people go to my church make my church somehow better, or 'righter' than a smaller church, since more people go there. Or, our pastor must know the scriptures better or interpret them better, since more people go there.

We see numbers as important building blocks for 'facts.' We want to know what percentage of people do something or another, and the greater the percentage the more we know that a particular 'fact' is true. We measure populations of behaviors and then determine how 'significant' these behaviors are, based on some quantifying formula that tells us the 'facts' about a behavior, or characteristic we are measuring. So, in many ways we give homage to king number.

"Those who accepted his message were baptized, and about 3,000 were added to their number that day."[71] "And the Lord added to their number daily those who were being saved."[72] "But many who heard the message believed, and the number of men grew to about 5,000."[73] "And the hand of the Lord was with them, and a great number of people believed and turned to the Lord."[74] "So the churches were strengthened in faith and grew daily in numbers."[75] I think these scriptures from the book of Acts get the idea across that if your church is not growing in numbers, you're doing something wrong. And I believe that many pastors and church planners get easily confused by these 'number' scriptures. So, these confused pastors think that the number of people in their congregations suggest they are on the right track and doing the work of the Lord. They must be right and the smaller churches wrong. These megachurches[76] must be the way to do things in the Christian world today.

We need a sense of perspective here. Israel began as a nation in the midst of a lot of much larger nations around them: Egypt, Assyria, Babylon, Greece, Rome. Christianity began as a 'sect' within much larger 'sects' around them: Judaism, Roman gods and emperor worship, paganism, Platonism, Islam, and sorcery. And in comparison, to the other religions and 'sects' around them, Christianity was small in numbers: but it was growing significantly.

"Brothers think of what you were when you were called. Not many of you were wise by human standards; not many were influential; not many were of noble birth."[77] And then in verse 28: "He choose the lowly things of this world and the despised things and the things that are not to nullify the things that are, **so that no**

---

[71] Acts 2:41; NIV

[72] Acts 2:47b; NIV

[73] Acts 4:4; NIV

[74] Acts 11:21; NIV

[75] Acts 16:5; NIV

[76] Defined as a church with over 2,000 members. But the prefix 'mega' is confusing. The prefix 'mega' means million not thousand; thousand would be kilo, so these 'megachurches' are really kilo-churches.

[77] 1 Corinthians 1:26; NIV

one may boast before him."[78] Does this sound to you that God is all about numbers: How many?

It wasn't until the Middle Ages that Christianity as a political alliance with kings and queens began to be a significant religion in the Western world. During most of this time the church was a tool of the kings and queens that ruled the Western world. The church was used as a means to an end to rationalize the importance of kings and queens and their right to rule. And at this point in history the numbers of the 'faithful' were important to the influence of the church and the political alliance that it enjoyed during this time.

The modern game of chess represents the influence of the church in the political life of the Western world. Chess was introduced into the Western world in the Middle Ages. It is believed to be a modification of an Indian game called chaturanga, a strategy game involving just military divisions. As it was modified in the West, it contained the bishop, a reference to the influence of the church in the politics of kings and queens.

And then later came the big events in the Christian church that lead to the Reformation. The Reformation is usually believed to have begun when Martin Luther tacked up his complaints of the Roman Catholic Church in 1517, but there had been many attempts at reformation of the Roman Catholic church before that, due to the corruption in the Roman Catholic Church at the time. One of the decisive things that caused Martin Luther's reformation being more influential is his translation of the Bible into German and the invention of the printing press. This allowed the 'common' folks the ability to read the Bible in their own language, their vernacular, rather than Latin. Before that, the Roman Catholic Church pretty much controlled how the 'people' interpreted the scriptures.

And again, what does this have to do with king number? Well, the greater number of people you have in your political group, the greater influence you have in what happens in the world. Because you are big in number, you must be big in importance, and big in changing the course of the world. So, very subtlety the importance

---

[78] 1 Corinthians 1:28; NIV

of numbers began to be a major factor in the political movements of the world. And the Reformation was the cause of a lot of 'sects' and denominations to form in the Christian Church. And the see-saw battle between politics and religion continued.

Fast forward to the Age of Enlightenment or Age of Reason that happened in the 1700's. This was the century of philosophy. Philosophers and scientists of this century widely circulated their ideas in printed books, journals, and pamphlets. There were meetings of scientific academies, Masonic lodges, literary salons, coffeehouses and the like. The populations were getting educated. The populations could read. Science became an important truth getting method. Remember that science is based on facts that contain numbers.

Then at the end of this Age of Reason came the well-known revolutions, particularly the American and French revolutions. These two seemed to spawn an Age of Revolution and later more revolutions: Chinese, Russian, Irish, Greek, Latin American, Serbian and many more minor ones. And in each case king number was important.

The revolution that was important to us Christians in America was the American Revolution. This started out as a minority group calling for revolution from Great Britain. What seemed important in this revolution taking hold in America was one pamphlet written by Thomas Paine, called "Common Sense." This essay caused a lot of people in America to change their minds and support the ongoing minority revolution that was in progress. And, in my opinion, with a lot of luck and some acts of Providence, we won the revolution and became the United States of America.

Even though the founding fathers and mothers of America, did their best to try to separate the church and the state, we have managed to keep this political alliance intact over the last 243 years of our history. And why? King number. Many Christians believe today that they can make the world more Christian by influencing as many politicians as they can to become more Christian in their thinking and bring in the Kingdom of God on earth, or bring about the Second Coming of Christ on earth, so they form political action committees and give big sums of money to politicians who 'promise' to take the Christian agenda and make it part of our government. And why? - king number again.

King number sits there in the 'back of our head' subtly influencing our thinking. Telling us how important numbers are if we are going to get anywhere as a religion, or way of thinking and being. But what we fail to get is that God is interested in only one number: ONE. God is interested in unity. God is interested in a **one-on-one** relationship with each **one** of us. How many times must we read this scripture before we finally get it? "My prayer is not for them alone. I pray also for those we will believe in me through their message, that all of them may be ONE, Father, just as you are in me and I am in you. May they also be in us so the world may believe that you have sent me. I have given them the glory that you gave me, that they may be ONE as we are ONE. I in them and you in me. May they be brought to **complete unity** to let the world know that you sent me."[79] Who is in charge of this unity, this ONE-ness? It certainly isn't any political group or 'sect' interested in king number.

This ONE-ness has a good word that is used in the New Testament. That word in Greek is *homothymadon*. This word is usually translated as 'together,' or 'of one accord.' But neither of those translations do this Greek word justice. They don't get to the full meaning of *homothymadon*. We are OK when we translate parts of the word, like homo- meaning 'the same.' Where we get off track is the middle syllable '*thyma.*' From what I can learn about this syllable, it means 'anger' or 'passion.' (In the uncombined form it is the Greek word '*thymos.*') Well, this syllable sure got my biology mind activated. We all have a thymus in the center of our chest above our heart. The name of the thymus comes from the Greek word (*thymos*), meaning "anger", or "heart, soul, desire, life", possibly because of its location in the chest, near where emotions are subjectively felt. So, there is a strong connection here. So, translating *homothymadon* as just 'of one accord' just doesn't do it for me. What is lacking is the intensity of the word. The English translation misses the 'fire' in the word

---

[79] John 17:20-23a. NIV; caps mine for effect. Bold type mine.

homothymadon. If I could do my own translation, I would translate it to mean: "they were all one accord and 'all fired up' about their life together. There was a passion and intensity to their ONE-ness. Another way to see it is that the early church was 'on fire' about their life together. Or as Peterson said so well: "There was something burning within those followers of Jesus, drawing them together in the same mind and spirit, something akin to the energy of anger, but without anger."[80] This is the ONE-ness that we miss when we just focus on king number. It's time to "Light the Fire Again!"[81]

"If God were more sensible, he'd take his little army and shape them up. Why, whoever heard of a soldier stopping to romp in a field? It's ridiculous. But even more absurd is a general who will stop the march of eternity to go and bring him back. But that's God for you. His is no endless, empty marching. He is going somewhere. His steps are deliberate and purposeful. He may be old, and He may be tired. But He knows where He is going. And He means to take every last one of his tiny soldiers with Him. Only there aren't going to be any forced marches. And, after all, there are frogs and flowers and thorns and underbrush along the way. And even though our foreheads have been signed with the sign of the cross, we are only human. And most of us are afraid and lonely and would like to hold hands or cry or run away. And we don't know where we are going, and we can't seem to trust God -especially when it's dark out and we can't see Him! And He won't go on without us. And that's why it's taking so long."[82]

---

[80] E. Peterson; *The Jesus Way;* Eerdman's Publishing Co.; 2007; p.262

[81] B. Doerksen; "Light The Fire Again;" Music Services Inc. 1994.

[82] Bell, Martin; *The Way of the Wolf, The Gospel in New Images;* Seabury Press; 1971; p. 92.

THE CLERGY[83]

As a father of a pastor, this topic can get me into a lot of trouble. But I will be as cautious as I can. I agree with Eugene Peterson, when he said: "Priests are at their best when we don't notice them."[84] What I think Peterson is getting at is that the true calling of a priest or pastor is humility. The clergy is to be transparent, or a reflection of God's light, not the source. He She simply points to the source of Light and Goodness: God. The pastor or priest keeps us focused in the right direction: Jesus.

But what has happened in the Church since Peter became the first clergyman: The first 'Pope?' Well, all you have to do is look at all the ceremony and liturgy and adornments that we see in churches today to understand what I mean. We have the robes, the collars, the vestments, the rituals, the pulpits, and the adoration of our pastors and priests in the churches of today. This doesn't seem to be too transparent, or reflective of God's light.

Many times, I have talked with fellow Christians about continuing in a community church where their adored pastor or priest has left, due to their favorite pastor moving to another community or being transferred somewhere else. Some of these fellow Christians have even stopped going to a church because of this change in pastor or priest. What has happened? What went wrong?

What went wrong was that we have elevated our pastors and

---

[83] The body of all people ordained for religious duties, especially in the Christian Church.

[84] E. Peterson; *The Jesus Way;* Eerdmans Publishing Co.; 2007; p.226.

priests to a higher level of human existence. We have elevated them to positions they did not know they were taking when they became 'ordained.' Sometimes these pastors and priests are seen as exemplar Christians who point the way to a better life, a higher calling, an example of a life lived in the presence of God. The fact is they are just as human and sinful as the rest of us 'run of the mill' followers of Jesus. And as a father of a pastor, I can attest to that. And some of these pastors and priests like it this way. They enjoy the adoration, the 'hanging on their every word,' their preferential treatment at various places of business and entertainment.

And what I am talking about is 'clericalism.' "Clericalism arises from an elitist and exclusivist vision of vocation, that interprets the ministry received as a power to be exercised rather than as a free and generous service to be given. This leads us to believe that we belong to a group that has all the answers and no longer needs to listen or learn anything. Clericalism is a perversion and is the root of many evils in the Church: we must humbly ask forgiveness for this and above all create the conditions so that it is not repeated."[85] I think Pope Francis was on the right track when he gave this definition of 'clericalism.' Did you notice that Pope Francis thinks the clergy should be a vocation of free and generous service that is a gift? And do you remember what St. Paul said about gifts? "Are all of you apostles? Are all prophets? Are all teachers? Do all work miracles? Do all have gifts of healing? Do all speak in tongues? Do all interpret?"[86] And then the next part of Paul's letter is the famous 1Corinthians 13 about how to love people. The Jesus community is made up of all kinds of gifts of service, not just one person who does it all for the church and we make them pastors and priests. And if you notice our pastors and priests have taken on many of these gifts in their vocation, even if they don't have them! And then we wonder why so many of them get 'burned out.'

Then there is the clericalism that Jesus faced when He was on earth: The Pharisees and the Sadducees. These two groups of people

---

[85] – Pope Francis; 2018 address to the synod on young people.
[86] 1 Corinthians 12: 29-30; NIV

were the pastors and priests of His day. He had a lot of harsh words of them. Probably the best example of Pharisees that we have in the Bible are Joseph of Arimathea, Nicodemus, and Gamaliel. These Pharisees took care of Jesus and listened to Him. And the worst of the Pharisees was in my mind Caiaphas: the high priest that condemned Jesus in the middle of the night at a 'kangaroo court' at his mansion in Jerusalem and then sent him to Pilate to be crucified. Caiaphas had all the trappings of a completely compromised, politically influenced religious leader, under the thumb of Rome and making a lot of money from his position as chief priest. The poster child of clericalism of his day.

Who then are the Caiaphas' of today? Who is it that makes a lot of money from their religion? Who is it that sells their religious products to thousands of people to support their lavish lifestyles and expensive tastes? I think you know the answer. I think you know who they are and what they are all about. Yet, the question remains: why do so many Christians follow them and hang on their every word, either in a book or at a church? My answer is this: clericalism has caused them to spring up all over the place. The so-called 'prosperity gospel' is so appealing to people that they will do whatever these false teachers tell them to do and buy the products these false pastors tell them to buy. It's all about me first and God second, and other people last.

There is also the 'Christians' in churches who encourage this 'clericalism' that I am referring to. These are the people who are trapped in ritual and preoccupied with outward form and regulations. These are the people who come to church for all the trappings of worship. I have experienced them in my life too many times. I remember once when I was the chairman of my local church's staff relations committee. I was the liaison between the clergy and professional staff in the church and the so-called 'lay people.' One morning after church I received a phone call from someone who remained anonymous and simply said to me: "The candles on the altar were not lit today, what are you going to do about it?" Then they hung up.

I soon found out this was only the tip of the iceberg of ritual worship at this church. I later learned that everything during the worship service needed to be 'right.' The flowers on the altar had to be just the right type; the choir robes had to be the 'right' color, and so forth. Then later when this church built a new sanctuary, I was astounded at all the important details that these 'Christians' wanted to make in order for their worship experience to be complete and 'perfect.' This was really a form of perfectionism that the Church of Jesus Christ can do without. All the trapping and rituals of worship are for one reason only: to point to God/Christ. And that is the calling of the pastors too.

I think that a lot of this virulent 'clericalism' that has infected the Church of Jesus Christ is the result of wanting to 'feel' good about ourselves. A lot of 'Christians' come to church for an hour or so of 'feeling' religious and pious and 'good.' They are dressed just right; behave just right; have all the right instruments of worship, so they must be doing 'church' right. But what they refuse to do is prostrate themselves before God. They refuse to have a 'contrite heart' and know that they are 'undone' in God's presence. "Just as I am, without one plea, but that Thy blood was shed for me. And that Thou bid'st me come to Thee; O Lamb of God, I come! I come! Just as I am, though tossed about, with many a conflict, many a doubt; fighting and fears within without, O Lamb of God, I come! I come! Just as I am, and waiting not to rid my soul of one dark blot. To thee whose blood can cleanse each spot, O Lamb of God, I come! I come!"[87]

And here is the point. We need to all be priests and pastors to each other. We ARE a priesthood of believers.

---

[87] Charlotte Elliot; 1835. This was the hymn that the well-known evangelist Billy Graham heard during his 'conversion' experience in **Charlotte** North Carolina (1934); almost a century later. He then used this hymn as his 'alter call' for many decades during his many 'crusades' from 1947 to 2005 when he retired. Notice the exclamation points.

GROW UP!

In the short book Ephesians, St. Paul is writing about the unity of the Church. In the fourth chapter of Ephesians he writes about the bond of unity that we Christians have with each other: To paraphrase he emphasizes – ONE: body, Spirit, hope, Lord, faith, baptism, God.[88] And then he writes this about Christ ascending and descending from heaven and earth in order to "fill the universe."[89] And then he goes on to say that we Christians are to prepare ourselves for service in order for the Church to be built up until we all- "reach unity in the faith and in the knowledge of The Son of God **and become mature** attaining to the whole measure of the fullness of Christ."[90] In more modern language: **Grow up!**

In *The Message*, Peterson interprets these verses more in our modern vernacular: "No prolonged infancies among us, please. We'll not tolerate babes in the woods, small children who are an easy mark for impostors. God wants us to grow up, to know the whole truth and tell it in love -like Christ in everything. We take our lead from Christ, who is the source of everything we do. He keeps us in step with each other. His very breath and blood flow through us, nourishing us so that we will **grow up** healthy in God, robust in love."[91]

The point I want to make is that we aren't very good at this growing up part of our faith. We like to stay 'babes in the woods' and

---

[88] See Ephesians 4: 3-6 NIV.
[89] Ephesians 4:10b NIV.
[90] Ephesians 4:13 NIV.
[91] Ephesians 4: 14-16 *MSG*

'small children' in our thinking. We like all the children stories in the Bible from the baby Jesus to being like little children so we can enter the Kingdom of heaven, when Jesus says: "I tell you the truth, unless you change and become like little children, you will never enter the kingdom of heaven."[92] So, we like to remain in a kind of infantile state, just worrying about our personal relationship with Jesus, like a little child just worrying about his or her relationship with mom and dad.

But then, how do you hold being like a little child with this verse? "I am sending you out like sheep among wolves. Therefore, be as shrewd as snakes and as innocent as doves."[93] I hope when you see these two Scriptures together you get the idea that maybe Jesus was telling us to have the innocence of children **and** the shrewdness of snakes in this world. In order to do that we must **grow up!**

Every one of us has a little child within. There have been many books written on getting in touch with your inner child.[94] This is the childlike person within us that we defend and protect from the world around us. But this immature person needs to **grow up!** We are no longer this child from our past. So, we need to find a balance between being innocence and shrewd.

Shrewd. This word basically means having sharp powers of judgement; synonym: astute. This word comes down to us from an old meaning of the word 'shrewd.' It originally meant a mischievous or malicious person. But then look at the ancient Greek meaning: practical wisdom; from the word *phronimos*. The New Testament uses this Greek word 8 times and it is usually interpreted as wise. Wise in practical ways.

In order to be wise in the ways of the world around you, you need to **grow up!** You need to be able to tell the truth from the lies that surround us each and every day. You need to be aware of the propaganda, advertisements, political messaging, half-truths in the

---

[92] Matthew 18:3 NIV.

[93] Matthew 10: 16 NIV.

[94] The childlike aspect of a person's psyche — typically, the personality and the memories of one's childhood.

LEARNING FORGIVENESS

In my way of thinking one of the most difficult things to 'grow up' in is how and when to forgive others who have wronged you. And who and when do others forgive you? We start out with this idea of forgiveness by learning (quite to our surprise) that forgiveness is reciprocal. We pray this every time we pray the Lord's Prayer: "Forgive us our trespasses (debts) *as* we forgive those who trespass (debtors) against us." The little word- as - is the reciprocal word. It's a two-way street. And Jesus emphasizes this part of the prayer right after he teaches it to the disciples.[95]

Then there are all those times that Jesus talks and applies the idea of forgiveness. Don't offer your gifts until you have 'reconciled' (forgiveness) your brother.[96] Or the idea of forgiving your brother or sister "seventy seven" times.[97] Peter had asked him should I forgive my brother seven times and Jesus uses a power of ten in reply: 10 times 7 times more than just 7, or some translations say 70 times 7; and that would be 490 times. And that's not the point. I think Peter used the number 7 because that was a sacred number in the Hebrew community. Seven meant completeness to the Hebrew of Jesus' time. For example, the seven days of creation when on the seventh day God rested. It was a number that figured in the Jubilee year:[98] It is a number that was used in the Bible at least 735 times. (A lot of

---

[95] Matthew 6:14-15 NIV
[96] Matthew 5:23-24 NIV
[97] Matthew 18:21-22 NIV
[98] Leviticus 25:8; NIV; read the whole chapter for details.

arithmetic here) So, I think Peter was saying seven times and then I'm done forgiving.

I think Jesus' point in all these numbers is we are to be a forgiving community, not using numbers to tally our forgiveness. We are not to quantify our forgiveness. Forgiveness is just what we are about. It is what God is about. And we are to behave as God behaves toward us. And the first step in learning forgiveness is to know that we need to be forgiven, not just once and for all, but every day we need to pray for our forgiveness. Then we know that our brother or sister needs forgiveness as much as we do. When the community of Jesus refuses to do this, it goes astray.

And God is very patient in our learning of forgiveness. Without humiliation we will not learn much about forgiveness. Growth toward wisdom and love is slow. Growth in how and when to forgive is very slow. The first step is humility. To know how much, we have been forgiven and how much forgiveness we need each day is the first step to forgiving others.

Step two for me is extending my forgiveness to others who I believe have wronged me. Not that they know they have offended me, or hurt me, but I perceive they have. They may not know they have. That does not mean that I go up to another person and say, "I forgive you." They may have no idea what I am talking about. Extending my forgiveness can mean refusing to continue an argument, or gossip about someone, or just saying 'hello' in a polite way. And it also can be a confrontation. We need to learn how to confront people who we believe have hurt or wronged us. This doesn't have to be an angry confrontation at all. Just simply stating how they have wronged or hurt you can be enough. And this is where the **as** part comes in. If they get what you are saying and they understand how they have hurt or wronged you, then they are likely to say something to the effect of "I'm sorry," or "I didn't know that bothered you." NOW reconciliation is happening. NOW forgiveness is happening.

Jesus spent His ministry on earth extending God's forgiveness to anyone and everyone He encountered, even at His crucifixion:

"Father forgive them, for they do not know what they are doing."[99] And doesn't that just sum up for us the problem we have? That almost all the time we do not know what we are doing when we hurt or wrong other people. We are usually massaging our need to be right or our need to be superior or our need to protect ourselves in some way either physically or emotionally. So, for me, forgiveness is tied in our unawareness of ourselves, our motives and our needs. Forgiveness is a life-long learning experience. And I don't think we will ever reach the level of forgiveness that Jesus had. I can't imagine forgiving people who had just nailed me to a cross. So, step three for me is learning to become more and more aware of my own failure to understand the world around me. More humility.

The first stone. I knew a pastor who kept a stone on his desk in his office. One day I asked him why that ordinary rock was on his desk. He told me that it was a reminder to him to not cast the first stone. At the time I was a new Christian and had no idea what he was talking about. He told me the story of Jesus and the woman caught in adultery.[100] The crowd around her wanted to stone her. Jesus wrote in the dirt and stood up and said; "If any one of you is without sin, let him be the first to throw a stone." The crowd, one by one, left so there was only Jesus and the woman caught in adultery. And then, Jesus being Jesus, said: "Woman, where are they? Has no one condemned you?" The stone on the pastor's desk reminded him of his need for forgiveness. He was no better or worse than the woman caught in adultery.

Step four: forgive and forget? Well, that's the adage. Well, there is nothing in the Bible about the forgetting part. You can't simply delete something from your memory. But you can take an attitude of no resentment about a wrong done to you. That is the forgiveness part. And you don't need to continue in relationship with someone who has hurt you and shows no signs of sorrow or repentance for what they have done to you. Did you get that? You can forgive someone and not relate to them. This is a very important idea for people who

---

99   Luke 23:34 NIV
100   John 8:1-11 NIV

were abused in childhood, or abused in marriage, or abused in the workplace by uncaring and insensitive people. Yes, there are evil people in the world. They are just part of the landscape. And you can tell them by their behaviors and 'fruits.'

"Watch out for false prophets. They come to you in sheep's clothing but inwardly they are ravenous wolves. By their fruits you recognize them." [101] After I wrote this, I realized it needs some unpacking in relation to forgive-ness. We tend to think this verse only applies to people who are prophets. People who are in the 'church.' The term 'false prophet' is used several times in the New Testament. I think more clarity of what it means is found in 2 Peter.[102] Here St. Peter tells us that there are not only false prophets but false teachers and put them in the same group of people; basically, people who deceive. People of the lie. And that gets to my point. We all have had people in our lives who lie, and some who lie compulsively. And sometimes these liars are our teachers and parents and relatives and 'friends.' The key is to recognize them by their 'fruits.' Now, this is another term that gets confusing.

What is a fruit? There are many ways to look at this term, either from a biological view or a metaphoric view. I think both views can be instructive. In biology a fruit is what a plant produces in order to reproduce. The fruit is the carrier of the DNA of that plant, so that the next generation of that plant can be. As a metaphor a 'fruit' is something that results from a person's behaviors and true goals in life. For example, my sons are both my carriers of my DNA and their lives show the 'fruits' of my parenting. And now you can 'see' the 'fruits' of my life in them. (Boy, that's a scary statement to me.) Anyway, I hope that gets my point across about 'fruits.'

So, when Jesus says you can tell them by their 'fruits,' he means that you can read their motives and goals in life by how they behave and act in the world. If these false prophets and teachers lie, belittle, backbite, mock and insult people, that is their 'fruits.' And the big 'fruit' is the lie. The big lie, told over and over. And if you confront

---

[101] Matthew 7: 15-16 NIV
[102] See 2 Peter 2: 1-3. NIV

them with your truth about what they have done to you and they show no signs of repentance or sorrow: Don't relate to them: Don't continue to let them have emotional time in your life. You can't forget them, but you can release them to a life-long learning experience of forgiveness.

ACCORDING TO YOUR WORD

"According to the Word of the Lord" or some variation of 'according to your Word,' occurs in the Bible about 50 times (or there about depending on translation). It only appears in the New Testament twice and both times in the book of Luke. Most of the usages of "According to the Word of the Lord," appear in the Old Testament. It seems to be an Old Testament usage, particularly the word 'according' which is used 793 times: 672 times in the Old Testament and 121 times in the New Testament. Most of the "According to the Word of the Lord" verses are in the books of 1Kings, 2Kings, Numbers, Psalms, and 1Chronicles.

So what? Well, in the books about the Kings of Israel, there is a lot of references as to whether a particular king obeyed the Word of the Lord or not. In the book of Psalms, the Word of the Lord is couched in the idea that God will honor his promises; "according to your Word." And all the uses of this phrase are in one Psalm; number 119, the longest Psalm in the Bible. To me, the important thing to note is why is this phrase is used only twice in the New Testament, and usually in only one translation? So, here they are.

"Behold the handmaid of the Lord; be it unto me according to thy word."[103] And then there is the 'nunc dimittis,' which is Latin for the prayer of Simeon: "Now dismiss Thy servant, O Lord, in peace,

---

[103] Luke 1:38; KJV

according to Thy Word."[104] Two ends of life's spectrum of age: a young virgin woman, and an old man: the beginning and end of life. What is often overlooked about these two moments is the being in the right place at the right time part of these statements. In all likelihood Mary, the mother of Jesus, was alone when the angel of God visited her. We don't know for certain, but since there was no comments or references to others being present, it is not a stretch to think that Mary was alone. I think that when we are alone that is when God most likely will send us a 'messenger' of some sort. In the case of Simeon, the right time and place is much clearer. Simeon "moved by the Spirit he went into the temple courts."[105] And this is followed by Simeon taking Jesus in his arms and pronouncing his 'nunc dimittis.'

Imagine that you are Mary and Joseph taking your newborn son into the temple to do "what the custom of the Law required."[106] In all likelihood this 'custom' was a purification of a mother, who had just had a baby. The Mosaic law required that the new mother appear at the temple and offer a sacrifice (usually two doves or young pigeons). This then makes her ceremoniously 'clean.'[107] You are entering the temple when this old man comes up to you and takes your son out of your arms and praises God. And then this old man (not a priest) starts to tell them all about who their son was and what He would do. Talk about a coincidence. And then on top of that this 'prophetess' named Anna comes up to you and tells you pretty much the same thing. And both these old people (Simeon and Anna) did this at the same time. Talk about coincidence. Talk about being in the right place at the right time.

Notice that both these people (Simeon and Anna), had been waiting most of their lives for this one moment, when Jesus' mother came to the temple in Jerusalem for a 'ceremonial cleansing.' And both these events were "according to your Word" events. Think

---

[104] Luke 2:29; KJV
[105] Luke 2:27a; NIV
[106] Luke 2:27b; NIV
[107] See Leviticus 15:29 NIV for more details.

about it. In the arms of Mary, rests the Word of God; Jesus. Both Simeon and Anna are waiting for the Word of God, and here He is. Everything comes together in one moment of time. The Word of God is revealed. The Word made flesh- According to Your Word.

And then there is Jesus the Christ: The Word. The Logos. How does Jesus, like his mother Mary, handle this "according to your Word?" Does He, because He is the Word, do what he wants? Does he summon angels to do his bidding? No. He prays "Your will be done." (Lord's prayer) He prays in the place called Gethsemane: "My Father, if it is not possible for this cup to be taken away unless I drink it, may your will be done."[108] According to whose Word? His mother's prayer in a different form. The intent is the same. It is God's Word who now gives in to the will of God.

And that is our stand too. As followers of Jesus we need to learn from Jesus, the Word made flesh, our need for humility before our Father, our Abba. Wait on God. Wait for His Word and His Will in our lives. We are servants. We 'wait upon the Lord.' Our patience as a people, loved beyond any human understanding, is to serve and wait: According to Your Word.

---

[108] Matthew 26: 39b; NIV

THE NAME

"What's in a name? that which we call a rose by any other name would smell as sweet."[109] A name. What's in a name? Well, then there is The Name. The Name of God: I AM; "Ego eimi" in Greek. The tetragrammaton in Hebrew: YHWH. Actually, the unspoken Name of God. The Name was meant to be kept silent. To be held in awe and reverence. Just to be. God was 'represented' in the Hebrew ark of the covenant as a blank space between the two golden cherubim.[110]

And then along comes Jesus to the Temple in Jerusalem at the feast of Tabernacles. He goes through a lot of debates with the Pharisees and Jews who were loyal to the Pharisees. (For details see John 7:14 through John 8:57.) And then at the end of chapter 8 Jesus uses The Name: "I tell you the truth," Jesus answered, "before Abraham was born, I AM!" And to the Pharisees that is blasphemy. This guy Jesus just made himself equal with God; YHWH. Did you get this? Jesus is claiming to be eternal; the Alpha and Omega, the beginning and the end, the firstborn of creation. He has always been and always will be. Talk about arrogance. Well, this did it for the Pharisees. What did they do next? They picked up stones to kill Jesus. And what did Jesus do? He did what he had done before; hid himself and 'slipped away.' And to me, it is the hiddenness that Jesus shows that proves who He is. Have you ever thought about 'how' Jesus could hide himself in a crowd that is about to kill him? Have you ever experienced a moment in time when you saw clearly

---

[109] W. Shakespeare; *Romeo and Juliet; Act II, Scene II.*
[110] A winged angelic being.

the glory of creation, or the mystery of a miracle? Have you had an ever so fleeting experience of being in the presence of God, and then suddenly it 'slipped away?' I think that was what it was like in the Temple in Jerusalem so long ago, when Jesus 'hid himself' and 'slipped away' from the temple grounds.

We hear such comments from clergymen as: "In the name of Jesus;" or "In God's name." Many times, the phrase "In the name of Jesus" is used in healings and the so-called exorcism of some demonic force said to be living in a person. Jesus, in the scriptures, seemed have no problem with removing whatever 'demon' or controlling 'spirit' was afflicting someone. He simply said: "Come out." And further, these 'evil spirits' seemed to know Jesus quite well.[111] So then, invoking a name seems to be as important in having events happen. Jesus also said; "From now on, whatever you request along the lines of who I am and what I am doing, I'll do it."[112] But notice that Jesus uses a disclaimer about using His name. You need to be in line with who Jesus was and His purpose in the world, in order to use His name.

And of course, that means you need to know Jesus' purpose in the world. What was He here to do? Well, St. Paul sums it up rather nicely: "For **everything, absolutely everything,** above and below, visible and invisible, rank after rank of angels -**everything** got started in him and finds its purpose in him. He was there before any of it came into existence and holds it all together right up to this moment."[113] And that is why the scripture is read in Hebrews: "In putting **everything** under him (Jesus the Christ), God left nothing that is not subject to him. Yet at present we do not see **everything** subject to him."[114] Did you notice the term 'everything' coming up over and over? That means that the entire universe (everything) will be under Jesus' control. Not just you and me and our friends, but the entire universe. Is your God big enough for that? Or is your god only interested in people like you: People who think the way you do, or

---

[111] See Mark 5:6-14 NIV
[112] John 14: 13 *MSG*. I use this translation for clarity
[113] Colossians 1: 15-16; *MSG;* (bold type mine)
[114] Hebrews 2: 8b NIV (bold type mine)

act the way you do, or have the same genetics as you do. Well, if your god is limited by a lot of qualifiers, then you do not know the God of Jesus the Christ. You have manufactured your god. You have made for yourself an idol of your imagination. Your god is way too small. And further: "Because of that obedience (the cross), God lifted him high and honored him far beyond **anyone or anything,** ever, so that **all created beings** in heaven and earth -even those long ago dead and buried – will bow in worship before this Jesus Christ, and call out in praise that he is the **Master of All**, to the glorious honor of God the Father."[115] Did you get 'the Name?' Jesus the Christ. That is why we sing the hymn: "Jesus, name above all names;" or from Handel's Messiah: "King of Kings and Lord of Lords," in the well-known Halleluiah Chorus. This is THE NAME.

And do you also think that this event is some time in the future? That some 'day' will come when we will all stand around God's throne, or in God's presence, and THEN we will 'see' Jesus become the King of Kings and Lord of Lords? Is this what you think? Well, if you do, you need to read the scriptures again. Did you notice that this is a process? That this began when Jesus was crucified and was resurrected. And today the process continues until "**all created beings** in heaven and earth" will finally bow before him, recognizing who He really is. The process has begun. It is going to its completion. You can't stop it. Jesus is already King of Kings and Lord of Lords. The problem is a lot of the universe does not know it. Us followers of Jesus know it. That is our calling; to tell what we know to be true.

Did you notice that king and lord are political titles- political names? These are words used for a political leader. Today, we would more likely use prime minister or president or a more modern term for a political leader. King and lord are archaic. These words were used in the past to denote a political leader. So, lets update the Halleluiah Chorus to "President of Presidents and Prime Minister of Prime Ministers." Not quite as poetic. Not quite as melodious. But closer to the Truth of who this Jesus is. He is our Commander in Chief. He is our Prime Minister. He is our President.

---

[115] Philippians 2: 9-11; *MSG*; (again bold type and parenthesis mine).

SYNCHRONICITY

This is a term that means "meaningful coincidences." Synchronicity was the word used by Carl Jung to describe events that occur with no causal relationship yet seem to be meaningfully related. Science describes these 'meaningful coincidences' as 'spurious correlations' or mere coincidences. Science explains these 'meaningful coincidences' as events that occur when you have a very large number of events,[116] any outrageous thing is likely to be observed, because we never find it notable when likely events occur, we highlight unlikely events and notice them more. Even if events occur that are highly unlikely to occur, science likes to think that these 'outliers' are within the realm of a statistical bell curve[117], though these 'meaningful coincidences' are at the very edge of the curve. And that nice and neatly explains synchronicity. Or does it?

When I took statistics in graduate school, the first thing that my professor said was: "Ladies and gentlemen there are three types of liars; liars, really bad lairs and statisticians." And, as I was soon to learn as I studied statistics, just how true this was. We learned how to minimize data and amplify data to make a point using statistics. There were all kinds of techniques to analyze data and help the data favor your particular viewpoint. And there were 'honest' and

---

[116] Attributed to Persi Diaconis and Frederick Mosteller.

[117] A **bell curve** (also known as normal distribution **curve**) is a way to plot and analyze data that takes the shape of a bell. In the **bell curve**, the highest point is the one that has the highest probability of occurring, and the probability of occurrences goes down on either side of the **curve**.

'dishonest' ways to organize your data to make a point. And today we have a world that looks for 'hard evidence,' many times using statistics to prove a point, neglecting many variables that are embedded in the data that has been collected. We are enamored with 'the facts.'

But back to synchronicity. Let me take an example from my personal life. I wrote a book, and had it published. It was 'online' and available to anyone on the internet. I have not done anything to advertise my book, and thought that only my friends and family would probably read it. In June 2019 I was in Denver, Colorado, on vacation, staying in a hotel not too far from the Denver airport. On Friday evening my wife and I did not feel like going out to dinner, so I suggested that I go over to a bar and grill across the street from our hotel and see what I could order for carry-out for our dinner. I sat at the bar and ordered a beer and looked over the menu for a suitable carryout. Usually when I was by myself, I spoke a silent prayer to God, letting God know I was available to whatever came my way. A woman came into the bar and sat right next to me. We started up a conversation. After a lot of conversation about our mutual travels around the world, our 'bucket lists' and the foreign countries that we had visited, and our mutual agreement of how our fellow 'countrymen' were very unaware of what was happening in the rest of the world, we began sharing about our families. I learned that she had lost a son to a heroin overdose. I listened to her pain, and expressed how I did not know how I would be able to deal with either of my sons dying. I suggested that she might be very angry at God. She hedged in her answer. I spoke about how God could handle our anger and that I was angry with God a lot. At some point I told her that I had written a book, addressing some of these issues. When she wrote down the title of my book, she looked at me and said: "Who are you?" I said that I was Don Poole. She said that her husband had read my book, and she could hardly wait to tell him who she talked to tonight.

Let me 'dissect' this story a little bit. This was obviously an 'outlier' event on a bell curve. In my mind this was way out on the very edge of the bell curve. The prob-ability of all these circumstances coming together in a bar in Denver on Friday evening is very random at best. If anyone wants to do the probability of all these events occurring in this bar in Denver, be my guest. As an estimate, I would guess that the probability is very low. And there is another way to look at this. Just maybe God arranged it. Maybe God orchestrated this meeting of the woman and I at the bar in Denver. In my mind, this is how God reveals himself to us. And the important thing to note is that God can have 'plausible deniability' in the event. His/her can remain hidden and then our choice is to believe that God either showed up or not. In other words, regardless of our belief system, we choose what we think happened in this very improbable event. We either choose faith in God, or faith in 'spurious correlations.'

I don't think this synchronicity is just isolated to personal events in our lives, even though I have been fortunate enough to have several of them in my life. I think that some our most celebrated Biblical events are just this form of synchronicity. I believe that if we Christians are willing allow this synchronicity of God to be His/Her hallmark, then maybe we can see God working more in our lives. Or as I used to say to my students: "When you least expect it, expect it." (of course, that's a whole other subject) Let me give one example and then list some more for your consideration.

Here goes: The Exodus. This is when the people of Israel were freed from the Pharaoh of Egypt and crossed the Red (or Reed) Sea on their way to the Promised Land. A big event for the Jewish people today, celebrated with Passover each year. Biblical scholars believe that this event happened around the 9th or 10th century BC. Since it is now 2019, that event would have happened around 2500 – 3000 years ago. Some Bible scholars place the Exodus as far back as 1500 BC, for a total of 3,500 years ago. None of these dates are exact and depend on time periods as they relate to forms of radiocarbon dating, archeological evidence, tree rings, ice samples, etc. So, the Exodus could have occurred as far back as 3,500 years ago, since the first five books of the Bible were not written down until around the 5th century BC (2,500 years ago). And remember that the history of the

Hebrews was 'carried' in human memory for many centuries before it was written down.

Where does this synchronicity come into play? Well, it seems that there was a significant eruption, known as the Minoan eruption, that was estimated to have happened around 3,500 years ago and this eruption caused the Minoan culture that flourished in the Mediterranean Sea to become devastated. The island of Thera, which is now known as Santorini, was the center of this eruption. This was one of the biggest volcanic eruptions known. It is believed that this eruption sent out a series of strange events and tsunamis that overwhelmed many of the cultures along the shores of the Mediterranean Sea. And one of those cultures at the time was Egypt. It seems possible that just as the Hebrews were crossing the Red Sea a tsunami was in progress. One of the things that happens before a tsunami wave hits is that the water recedes and could even become 'dry land' as described in the book of Exodus.[118]And then, when Pharaoh's army pursues the Hebrews the tsunami wave strikes. Of course, there is no way to prove this idea, but it does give a plausible way for the miracle of the crossing of the Hebrews over the Red Sea and the destruction of Pharaoh's army some explanation. God knew the timing of events, and Moses trusted God. Moses was in relationship with God even if the Hebrews were not. Fortunately, they listened to Moses and crossed the Reed Sea[119]. The important thing to notice here is the exact timing of events.

As you read the account of the crossing of the Reed Sea in the book of Exodus you will find a lot of other miraculous events occurring that can't be explained with just this synchronicity of events I have described. Remember that many centuries passed before this was written down, and this crossing of the Reed Sea is a founding event for the people of Israel. That is why it is celebrated today at Passover. As you read through the Bible there are many references to this crossing of the Reed Sea. If you want to check them

---

[118] Read Exodus 14; NIV; particularly verses 15 -18.
[119] Yam Suph in Hebrew; literally 'reed sea.' Where this was is disputed.

out, I have listed some of them in a footnote[120]. However, when this Exodus event is remembered, what is remembered is the basic fact: The Hebrews crossed the Reed Sea on dry land and Pharaoh's army is destroyed.

What happens to a founding story when centuries pass, and the story is not written down? Well, frankly, the story gets changed. We humans like stories to be rememberable and meaningful, so sometimes we either embellish them or fill in missing 'pieces' of information, through a process called confabulation.[121] These are not attempts to lie, but to give greater significance and completeness to a story. Over centuries these memories can change. That is just a basic understanding of human memory, and in no way reduces the significance of the founding event of Exodus. The basic 'fact' remains, and so does God's synchronicity. And it was God who acted, because of the arrangement of events. After all, God is the Creator of the universe and has all knowledge of events from the very beginning to the present. I think God can cause events to happen very precisely and we would have no way of proving it was God. In my way of thinking, God likes to remain hidden so that we can have freedom to be.

But don't get me wrong here. I can't explain the other miraculous events that were present at the Exodus, and I am not trying to make God's actions at the Exodus less significant than they were; my point is that God can carry out his will for us as a people and individually though these synchronous events. I am not trying to reduce the significance of the other miraculous events during the exodus, just pointing out God's timing in them.

As you may know by now; timing is extremely important in life. One of the first questions we ask about doing a significant event in our lives is the timing. Is this the right time to get married? Is this

---

[120] Deuteronomy 11:4; Joshua 2:10; Psalms 66:6; 78:53; 106:7 & 9; 136: 13 & 15; Nehemiah 9:11; Acts 7:36; I Corinthians 10:1-2; Hebrews 11:29. NIV
[121] a memory error defined as the production of fabricated, distorted, or misinterpreted memories about oneself or the world, without the conscious intention to deceive.

the time to run for a political office? Is this the right time to buy a stock? And so forth. Timing is one of the first questions we ask ourselves in big decisions (hopefully). Doesn't it make sense that God's timing is what we want to pay attention to? Isn't listening to the promptings of the Spirit what we are taught to do? When God gives the 'go ahead' that is when we act. And then, if our timing is right (or synchronous) with God's, then events turn out for the best. "And we know that in all things God works for the good of those who love Him, who have been called according to his purpose."[122] Notice the two conditions that show that God is in them: 1) loving God; 2) according to His purpose. When we are aligned in our timing with these two conditions, synchronicity happens.

Some other stories in the Bible that I think are synchronous events are:

1. The falling of the walls in Jericho.[123] Jericho has been a city for thousands of years and is still active today. It was probably was first settled about 12,000 years ago. It was known for all the palm trees that surrounded the city. Some of its walls could have been there for thousands of years before Joshua and the Israelites showed up. The present-day position of the Jericho in the Bible is called Tel es-Sultan: a mound of rubble. Of course, there is a lot of speculation and lack of evidence about this event recorded in the Old Testament. But it is possible that when the Israelites got to this city the walls were in considerable dis-repair. And the timing was right for sound waves to finish them off.

2. Gideon's defeat of the Midianites.[124] Gideon (Jerub-Baal) had a message from the Lord for Gideon to go down to the Midianite camp and listen to what the Midianites were saying. And what do you know; just as he got there, he heard

---

[122] Romans 8:28 NIV

[123] See Joshua 6 in the Old Testament. Also read the 3 verses beforehand for perspective. Any version

[124] Judges 7 in the Old Testament.

two men talking about a dream that one of them had about a loaf bread rolling into their camp and collapsing a tent. Then Gideon carries out his plan to smash jars that were hiding the torches that 300 men surrounding the Midianite camp were holding. Then all the men blew their trumpets. The sudden surprise, in the middle of the night terrified the armies in the camp and they all fled. And in the confusion, they turned on each other, killing each other. Quite a string of coincidences. Fear is a powerful motivator. And again, the timing was just right for the events that happened.

3. Sennacherib's (Assyrian king) army of 185,000 men killed by an 'angel' of the Lord in the night. Again, a string of coincidences between the prophet Isaiah, Hezekiah (king of Judah) and Sennacherib. And the word 'angel of the Lord' in Hebrew is Malak. If you look up the meaning of what an 'angel of the Lord' can do, or appear, or accomplish, you get into a lot of definitions and opinions and theories about 'angels' and their manifestations. It is likely that this 'angel of the Lord' in 2 Kings chapter19, could be a disease or pestilence that affected all the 185,000 men in Sennacherib's army. Maybe they all ate the same kind of rotten food in their camp. That is not what is important. What is important to me is the timing of events: again.

I think there are many more synchronous events in the Bible that can't be proven one way or another. To me, what is important is the timing of these events coming together at the same point in time and place. I don't have any idea how God arranges these synchronous events; I just **choose to believe** that God does.

WHO'S ON FIRST?[125]

"We follow this sequence in Scripture: The first Adam received life; the Last Adam is a life-giving Spirit. Physical life comes first, then spiritual – a firm base shaped from the earth, a final completion coming out of heaven. The First Man was made out of earth, and people since then are earthy, the Second Man was made out of heaven, and people now can be heavenly. In the same way that we've worked from our earthly origins, let's embrace our heavenly ends. I need to emphasize, friends, that our natural, earthy lives don't in themselves lead us by their very nature into the kingdom of God. Their very 'nature' is to die, so how could they "naturally" end up in the Life kingdom?"[126]

Now, let's look at these verses in the NIV version. "If there is a natural body, there is a spiritual body. So, it is written: "The first man Adam became a living being," the last Adam, a life-giving spirit. The spiritual did not come first, but the natural, and after that the spiritual. The first man was of the dust of the earth, the second man from heaven. As was the earthly man, so are those who are of the earth, and as of the man from heaven, so also are those who are of heaven. And just as we have borne the likeness of the earthly man, so shall we bear the likeness of the man from heaven."

In both these versions of the text from 1 Corinthians, there is a lot of first and lasts going on. So, the 'first' thing we need to clear

---

[125] This refers to a famous comedy routine by Abbott and Costello called "Who's on First." Look it up. It's very funny.

[126] Paul in 1 Corinthians 15: 45-50; MSG.

up is who is the first and who is the last. Paul is referring to the first human being according to the Bible: Adam. The last Adam is Jesus the Christ. And then there are those double references Paul uses: physical first, spiritual last. If you look at these first and last references the way I do, then you will see that this is a sequence of what has happened in creation of us humans and the Christ Event; the life and death of Jesus. The verse from the Old Testament that Paul quotes in part is "The first Adam became a living being." This is from Genesis 2: 7. But if you look at the verse in your Bible, it probably reads; "the Lord God formed the man from the dust of the ground and breathed into his nostrils the breath of life, and the man became a living being." Or something to the same effect. Notice that Paul does not use the verse word for word, and that is important to note. In the Orthodox Jewish Bible this part of Genesis 7:2 reads; "and the Adam became a nefesh chayyah." Whoa! What is a 'nefesh chayyah?' And this is the way Paul probably read it. A 'nefesh chayyah' is a soul- nefesh; living thing- chayyah. So, if we look at it this way the verse would read: "and the Adam became a soul living thing. A little awkward, but to the point. So what? Well in my way of thinking God did something extra with the first human; he was not only a living thing, but had a soul. Since a lot of people don't like the word soul because of its cloudy meaning, let's use the word spiritual. We all seem to get along with that word. So then, Adam had a spiritual nature tagged onto him that the other living things did not get from God. This verse in my way of thinking is a hinge in the scriptures which will determine how you see the creation story and the Christ Event of Jesus.

So then, what came first was a living thing with a spiritual nature- the adam. Now for the hard part. "The Holy Spirit will come upon you, and the power of the Most High will overshadow you. So, the holy one to be born will be called the Son of God."[127] Mary, Jesus' mother, had a 'spiritual being' in her womb. Again, a combination of Spirit and human, like the first adam, but here the importance in this human is Holy Spirit. Well, here is where a lot of people get all

---

[127] Luke 1: 35 NIV

hung up in their thinking. We like to argue about the 'virgin birth' and did Jesus really not have a human father, etc. Here is another way to look at it. If God added a spiritual nature into the first man, isn't it just as possible that he added a human nature into his Son? And if you notice they both are 'hidden' in the Scriptures. In summary: We are living things with a spiritual nature and Jesus was a Spiritual thing, with a human nature. Jesus was both all Spirit and all human. And just so you know, there are many forms of life on this planet that don't need a male to reproduce. Look up parthenogenesis. No, stop right now and look it up.

So far, so good? Then Paul tells us to "embrace our heavenly ends." In other words, focus on our spiritual nature and not on our physical nature. Why? Because that is where we are going; that is our endpoint. That is our teleology[128] (if you want to get verbose). We are all going toward our spiritual natures and not our physical natures. We are pilgrims on this planet and our true home is with God. That should be our focus. "Do not store up for yourselves treasures on earth, where moth and rust destroy, and where thieves break in and steal. But store up for yourselves treasures in heaven, where moth and rust do not destroy, and where thieves do not break in and steal. For where you treasure is, there your heart will be also."[129] Sounds to me that Jesus knew about entropy and the ephemeral[130] nature of our lives. So then, Jesus tells us to focus on the same things that Paul tells us to focus on: "our heavenly ends."

Now 'heaven' is another term we get all messed up with. The word heaven originally meant (in Greek) -sky, or a higher place (like the sky). But that is not how we think of the word 'heaven.' I think most 'Christians' think of heaven as a realm where God lives with his angels and where Jesus the Christ is on a throne of some sort next to his Father (God). Some 'Christians' think that this is a place where

---

[128] An explanation of phenomena in terms of the purpose they serve rather than from the cause of which they arise: Or the function of something's end purpose.

[129] Matthew 6: 19-21 NIV

[130] Lasting a very short time.

the devil fell from (and some of them can even tell you the day!). So, heaven is 'some place' up there, that we can't see until we die.

But what if you took it to mean just a 'higher place,' like a different dimension, or even a dimension where you can see God face to face? Not really caring what 'heaven' looks like, or whether it has golden brick streets and heavenly music and all the trappings that we like to imagine 'heaven' is like. What if 'heaven' is just where we can be in God's presence all the time? Is that still as appealing to you? Some people think 'heaven' is a place where we worship God continuously, and sing continuously his praises. Do you really think that is all there is to it; this thing called 'heaven?'

We have a lot of scriptures to tell us that 'heaven' is like what many 'Christians' believe with all the gold and singing and such. There are the stories about the heavenly banquet and the prophets of the Old Testament being in the 'throne room' of God, with the seraphim and cherubim. To me, the one thing all of these stories have in common is that the people involved are in the presence of God. How it looks and what it is like is the subject of much debate, and in my way of thinking, kind of pointless. The important thing for me is to be in God's presence.

"No eye has seen, no ear has heard, no mind has conceived what God has prepared for those who love Him; but God has revealed it to us by His Spirit."[131]

"One thing I ask of the Lord, this is what I seek: that I may dwell in the house of the Lord all the days of my life, to gaze upon the beauty of the Lord and to seek Him in His temple."[132]

---

[131] 1 Corinthians 2: 9-10 NIV

[132] Psalm 27: 4 NIV

JUBILATION

"Count off seven Sabbaths of years – seven times seven years: Seven Sabbaths of years adds up to forty-nine years." And then the 50th year becomes a Jubilee (or Jubilee) year. So, what is this thing called a Jubilee year and what then is jubilation? The word jubilee is used 22 times in the Old Testament, but not once in the New Testament. And so, what is the significance of this term in our thinking as Christians?

Jubilation is from a Latin term meaning 'to shout for joy.' It is a form of rejoicing. "Rejoice in the Lord always. I will say it again: Rejoice!"[133] Notice the exclamation point: a shout of joy. This word is associated with the Jubilee year in the book of Leviticus. A year of rejoicing in the Lord. A year when slaves were freed, land returned to original owners, and land was not to be cultivated. A year of rejoicing in the Lord. A year of renewal. A year when Israel remembered that it was God who owned everything and not them.

As Christians we need to take this meaning of jubilation and Jubilee into consideration in our daily lives. Every-thing we have belongs to God. We didn't bring anything into this world and we surely will not take anything out when we die. And we are to rejoice in this knowledge. We are to shout for joy, knowing that we are God's people. We belong to Him and He is the source of all we have.

"Shout for joy to the Lord, all the earth, burst into **jubilant song** with music; make music to the Lord with the harp, with the harp

---

[133] Philippians 4:4 NIV.

and the sound of singing, with trumpets and the blast of the ram's horn; shout for joy before the Lord, the King."[134] When do we burst into jubilant song? When we run out of words. When we sing like a baby babbling to its mother. When we know we are in the presence of the unknowable God. There is nothing left for us to do, but jubilate. You hear this kind of jubilant singing in some of our praise songs in church services. They write the lyrics for all of us to sing together, but that's not really what is going on. For example; in the song "I Shall Sing,"[135] there are at least 4 lines of just "la, la, la, la, la, la, la, la." They occur before and after every verse with words. You can find many other songs both Christian and spiritual that have similar lyrics. In my way of thinking these are examples of jubilant song within the lyrics that are a form of praise. It is what happens when we run out of words.

And then there is the big problem of language. "Language, unlike more intuitive, musical, forms of communication, is the perfect medium for concealing, rather than revealing, meaning."[136] In other words, it is easier to lie with words than it is with music. It is much harder to lie in song. Songs and music depend on intonation, pitch, intensity and syntax to get the message across. Language does not. How much propaganda do you hear sung? Not much. The only ones I can think of are advertisement jingles. A chanting slogan is the closest you get to music being used in propaganda. So, when we jubilate, we sing and shout and use nonsense syllables. And we more likely tell the truth. We more likely are in the Truth.

"Awake my lute, and struggle for your part with all your art. The cross taught all wood to resound His name, who bore the same.

---

134 Psalm 98: 4-6. NIV
135 Garfunkel, A. "I Shall Sing;" Columbia Records; 1973.
136 I. McGilchrist; *The Master and his Emissary;* Yale University Press; 2009; p. 106

His stretched sinews taught all strings, what key is best to celebrate this high day."[137] This is a different form of jubilation. This is the jubilation of the heart when it knows the meaning of the cross of Jesus the Christ.

---

[137] G. Herbert; "Easter" Everyman's Library; 2004 p. 23. This poem was originally published in around 1633 AD! I have taken liberties in the exact wording to make it more readable in our modern vernacular. Notice the pun on the word 'taught.'

NOT OF THE WORLD

MESSIAH

What is a messiah? Well, there are messiahs and then there is The Messiah. In the lesser use of the term messiah, it means someone who is an 'anointed one,' or a priest or king, who 'saves' people from something or brings about a new way of living and/or being. For example, a king of the Persian empire in the Old Testament was called a messiah.[138] The Hebrew text calls this king a messiah because he decreed that the Jews could return to Jerusalem and rebuild the temple. Then there is the term in Christianity: The Messiah -The Son of God; the Christ; Jesus. This is The Messiah who does it all. He is the Anointed King of the Jews. If you notice in the book of Matthew the wise men came looking for the new 'king of the Jews' to be born and what was written on the cross of Jesus? You guessed it: the king of the Jews in Latin, Aramaic and Greek, the three languages used in Jerusalem at the time of Jesus' crucifixion.[139] Like two bookends in the life of Jesus the Christ. The MESSIAH. The Anointed King.

So, if you are a Christian, or a follower of Jesus I think you need to choose some things about The Messiah.

1. Do you believe in the Jesus of history or the Jesus of metaphysics? Wait a minute, what is this thing called 'metaphysics?' Metaphysics is a branch of philosophy that

---

[138] See Isaiah 45:1 NIV. Here the term messiah in Hebrew is translated 'anointed one.'

[139] John 19:19-21 NIV. John is the only gospel of the four that adds this detail.

examines the fundamental nature of reality. So, if you believe in a Jesus of metaphysics, you believe the important part of Jesus' life was how he saved you and the rest of humanity from your sin. On the other hand, if you believe in a Jesus of history, then you believe that he is apocalyptic (inserted into time as a revelation from God). Then you understand that if He is the MESSIAH, then He is a revolutionary. He began a revolution called the Kingdom of God. And the sovereignty of God became human history. And by the way, this includes your personal salvation.

2. Do you believe in a Jesus as the Church, or Jesus the prophet? If you believe in Jesus as the Church, then you believe in keeping our institutions alive by accepting that we will have to 'live with' violence in our culture and hopefully gradually reduce it. You believe that we live by grace alone and we can't act in history. You believe we just wait for history to go on with the goal of 'progress' in making the world more 'Christian.' If you believe in Jesus as the prophet, then you believe in God's demand for 'perfection' and that Jesus' Sermon on the Mount **is** an institution that permits new beginnings, because Jesus **is** the Messiah.

3. Do you believe that the reign of God is internal of external? If you believe that the reign of God is internal, then you believe that your faith in God is private and subjective. Since there was no 'end time' right after Jesus death, then there must only be a subjective reign of God: God reigns in my heart, for example. If you believe that the reign of God is external then you believe that the Kingdom of God is a social order and not hidden. The Kingdom is a 'city on a hill.[140]' The Kingdom of God is a NEW way to do things.

4. Do you believe that the Church of Jesus the Christ is political or sectarian? Again, what is this thing called 'sectarian?' This refers to a form of prejudice, discrimination, or hatred arising from attaching relations of inferiority and superiority

---

[140] Matthew 5:14-16. NIV

to differences between subdivisions within a group. In other words, it is how we got to this point where we have all these denominations and 'sects' in Christianity today. When we believe that the Church of Jesus the Christ is sectarian, we believe in setting up dichotomies like science vs. religion; revelation vs. fact; protestant vs. Roman Catholic; etc. If you believe in a Church that is political then you believe in an alternative social group of resident aliens, called the Kingdom of God that is IN the world today. When Jesus rejected the use of the sword[141], feeding the world[142], and not taking the temple and Jerusalem by force[143], this WAS politically relevant! God will have the Kingdom come one small act at a time- not with force or violence.

5. Do you believe that your faith in Jesus is personal or social? If you believe that your faith in Jesus is personal, then you just keep it to yourself and only share it with friends who are willing to listen to your personal 'testimony.' You become an 'apologetic' for your faith. Again, what is this thing called 'apologetic?' This is the religious discipline of defending religious doctrines through system-atic argumentation and discussion. In other words, you kind of apologize for what you believe is true, though argument and discussion- a religious 'chat room.' If you believe that your faith in Jesus is social, then you believe that your faith in Jesus is within a forgiving, healing call to all humanity integrated into the Church. You don't apologize for what you believe, you simply state it. That is why we have the Apostle's creed and it's like. In the light of the resurrected crucified agape of Jesus the

---

[141] Various verses: Matthew 26:52 NIV; John 18:11 NIV. You need to be careful in the use of the term 'sword.' It is also used as a metaphor in the Bible.

[142] Matthew 4:1-4 and Matthew 14:22-23 NIV; John 6:14-15. Notice the word 'immediately' in Matthew 14: 22.

[143] Matthew 4:5-7 NIV; Matthew 21:6-17. Notice Jesus left the temple and went to another city: Bethany.

Christ, it is not a lack of good sense (as a lot of philosophy would tell you), or a weakness (as a lot of other religions see it) but the wisdom and power of God.[144]

So, what were your choices about THE MESSIAH. Do you still think Jesus is THE MESSIAH? You need to choose where you **stand** in relation to who Jesus is. For that makes all the difference in where you place your loyalties and allegiance. "Therefore, put on the full armor of God, so that when the day of evil comes, you may be able to **stand** your ground, and after you have done everything, to **stand**. **Stand firm** then..." (1 Corinthians 6:13-14a NIV)

---

[144] 1 Corinthians 1:22-25. NIV.

FALLOUT

There is a video game called "Fallout."[145] This game is based on the idea that the world has gone through a nuclear war and the earth is now a destroyed radioactive world, where life has been mutated into large, venomous creatures who roam free and humans are walled up into what is left of cities and towns. Everyone has chosen a group to belong to for their own personal safety in numbers. This game 'spawned' a lot of other games based on this nuclear war that would occur in 2077 AD. The term 'fallout' comes from the idea that after a nuclear war, residual radioactive material propelled into the upper atmosphere following a nuclear blast, "falls out" of the sky after the explosion and the shock wave has passed.

So, what does this have to do with Christianity? Well, we have a world that has 'fallout' from not understanding what 'sin' is. In fact, we have relegated this term to the dustbin of our vocabulary. When you use this word now, you are almost invariably marked as a Bible thumper or fundamentalist and put in the category of the unenlightened. If you are a science person, other science people just 'roll their eyes.' The Urban Dictionary describes sin as "good, dirty fun." In fact, by that definition sin is put in the realm of 'good,' but dirty. Dirty is defined as: " sexually exciting or explicit." Well, that certainly is a long way from the original meaning.

In the New Testament the word sin in Greek is *hamartia,* which literally means 'to miss the mark,' as an archer would miss the

---

[145] A series of post-apocalyptic role-playing video games created by Interplay Entertainment. 1997-2004.

bullseye. Again, that is a long way from what we think of when we think of the word 'sin' today. Many Christians today don't think of sin in the missing the mark sense, but in the catalog of sins sense. What I mean by that is that they have developed a catalog of 'sins' that they need to avoid in order not to 'sin.' When they violate one of these cataloged 'sins' they then see a need to confess. "Forgive me Father, for I have sinned:" and then list the sins committed since their last confession. And that isn't what the original intent of the word was anyway.

When I was a kid, we used to pray a prayer right before communion in which we said: "We acknowledge and bewail our manifold sins and wickedness, which we, from time to time, most grievously have committed, by thought, word, and deed, against thy Divine Majesty."[146] And boy did I get stuck on the word manifold, since my father was an automobile mechanic. All I could imagine is a car engine and its wicked manifold.[147] Again, a long way from the original intent of the word 'sin.' What struck me about this 'prayer of contrition' was the catalog idea and the idea that I only did this 'from time to time,' not all the time. So, that means to me that there were times that I did not 'sin.' I had a good shot at being 'perfect;' without sinning.

But let's go back to the original meaning of 'sin:' to miss the mark. This implies that this is a state of being. I shot my arrow and it missed the mark. There is not much I can do about it now. I just missed the bullseye. I came up short. "For all have sinned and fall short of the glory of God."[148] Fits nicely doesn't it? We have all 'fallen short,' missed the mark. We are in this state of sin. It's not a catalog, it's not a 'from time to time' thing; it is a state of being. I am and will continue to be a sinner. All I can do is ask for forgiveness as I forgive those who miss the mark with me.

Because we fail to understand the impact of sin in our lives,

---

146 The Act of Contrition from the Anglican Communion Service.
147 The manifold is a part of an engine where the exhaust gases or gas mixture is collected on top of an engine.
148 Romans 3:23a; NIV

we have fallout. "We have, it turns out, one of the best working democracies in the world, but the social results are far from encouraging. Our citizens are given votes and influence and freedom. And they are conspicuous across the board for living badly, frivolously, addictively, and selfishly."[149] We Americans think that 'sin' is not what is wrong with the world, but a lack of money; so, what do we do? We make more money to be 'prosperous.' We make more and more and consume more and more. We become the most prosperous nation in the world so that our citizens can 'pursue happiness' and "ensure domestic tranquility" and secure the "Blessings of Liberty,"[150] and the fallout is dishonesty, exploitation, pride and arrogance. These are the very things that 'fall short' of the glory of God. So, then knowing what 'sin' is is a very important understanding in Christianity. It is one of the hinges of our faith in God. We must realize that we are sinners, people who sin on a regular basis, and not from time to time or just from a personal list of 'sins.' We are a people who have 'missed the mark' and fallen short of the glory of God. Simply put: we are NOT God.

And Jesus said: "If anyone of you is without sin, let him be the first to throw a stone at her."[151] Notice the singular in the word 'sin;' not 'sins.' And again St. Paul: "The moment that I decide to do good, sin is there to trip me up. I truly delight in God's commands, but it's pretty obvious that not all of me joins in that delight. Parts of me covertly rebel, and just when I least expect it, they take charge."[152] And later in verse 24 of Romans 8 Paul says: "Who can save me from this **body of death?**"[153] Note 'body of death;' doesn't sound like a catalog of sins, or a now and then thing, this sin that Paul refers to. Sounds rather permanent to me. We need to get over thinking we can

---

[149] Peterson, Eugene; *Christ Plays in Ten Thousand Places*; Eerdmans Publishing Co.; p. 317.

[150] Phrases from the Declaration of Independence and the Preamble to the Constitution of the United States.

[151] John 8:7b. NIV

[152] Romans 7:21-23; *MSG*.

[153] Romans 7:24b. NIV (for effect)

avoid 'sinning.' We need to get over thinking we can 'be perfect.' We can't. In fact, perfectionism has no place in the Jesus Community.

"This is why perfectionists so often become workaholics; by ignoring the **ubiquity of sin** they persist in the illusion that if they accomplish just one more mission, master just one more act of devotion, successfully avoid contamination with just one more sloppily living Christian, get one more program up and running, they will emerge head and shoulders above all others. Some of them accomplish impressive projects and manage stunning achievements, but they also end up without friends, often without family, without forgive-ness because they never need it, and without love. Perfectionism assumes tragic proportions when an entire community is infected."[154]

And some of our Christian communities are infected with this perfectionism, because they assume that they can overcome 'sin.' There is only ONE person who has overcome 'sin' and that is Jesus the Christ. And again, where are we? At the foot of the cross, where we can lay down the burden of perfectionism and ask for forgiveness again, and again and again. Jesus Christ, Son of God, have mercy on me, a **sinner.**

---

[154] E. Peterson; *Christ Plays in Ten Thousand Places*; Eerdmans's Publishing Co.; 2005; p.320.

NATURE

John Muir was also known as "John of the Mountains" and "Father of the National Parks." He was an influ-ential Scottish American naturalist, environmental philosopher, glaciologist, author and early advocate for the preservation of wilderness in the United States of America. He helped found the Sierra Club. There is even a 'John Muir' day celebrated in Scotland.

To John Muir, nature was God. Muir beheld the violent beauty of God as reflected in nature. He, like all of us, was without excuse.[155] The 'trick' is identifying the source of this beauty; the supreme Good. "Why call me good, (Jesus said) the father alone is good."[156] Even Jesus pointed to the source of goodness and beauty: God alone, the creator of earth and sky, sunrise and sunset, bear, dragon fly, elk, magpie, glorious wildflowers, mountain peaks, serene lakes and even us ruinous creatures, bent on taming them all.

John Muir knew the simplicity of unified thought that he had gained through long times of solitude, that purified his point of receptivity. He knew the unity of contemp-lation, where left and right brain hemispheres work in harmony, the senses mediating their input for under-standing the pure act of existing, achieving a shared intimacy with nature, or as he so eloquently put it: "and throughout the whole of their beautiful lives (referring to a bird called the water ouzel), interpreting all that we in our unbelief call terrible in the

---

[155] See Romans 1:20 NIV
[156] Matthew 19: 17 NIV

93

utterances of torrents and storms, as only varied expressions of God's eternal love."[157]

John Muir knew that nature was God's mediating reality. The image of being, knowing and loving joined in one simple act. God's grace does not destroy or contort the natural world, but brings it to completion. God's grace takes our natural selves to the place of the 'supernatural' because in this grace we find ourselves in the presence of what is most consistently there in nature: God. Here the words of Jesus gain a new clarity we did not see before. Muir describes this experience of being while in the midst of a windstorm in the mountains of California. As the windstorm abated and he had participated in the high gale, he left his perch, from where he viewed the storm and wrote: "I beheld the countless hosts of forests hushed and tranquil towering above one another on the slopes of the hills like a devout audience. The setting of the sun filled them with amber light, that seemed to say, while they listened, "My peace I give to you.""[158] Here the words of Christ to his disciples before he went back Home, gives new meaning to the word 'peace.' The final word in the union of being, knowing and loving is "peace be unto you." And in the final act of our lives we rest in peace, God's peace given to us when the windstorm of life is over.

Nature is God's 'mediating reality.' Did you get that? To mediate is to intervene between people in a dispute in order to bring about an agreement or reconciliation. We sometimes use the word arbitration. So, nature serves as an arbitrator between God and us. Nature brings us to reverence. When we witness the beauty of nature, we see the beauty of God.

Nature serves also to show us our connectivity to the universe. We like to think that we are connected through our smart phones and computers through the technology of wi-fi and the like, but that is only one of the ways we are all connected. Nature connects us to the universe. John Muir knew of this connectivity when he wrote:

---

[157] E. W. Teale, editor; *The Wilderness World of John Muir*; Houghton Mifflin Co.; 1982; p. 161
[158] Ibid; p. 190.

"But if we should ask these profound expositors of God's intentions; How about those man-eating animals – lions, tigers, alligators -which smack their lips over raw man? Or about those myriads of noxious insects that destroy labor and drink his blood? Doubtless man was intended for food and drink for all these? Oh no! Not at all! These unresolvable difficulties connected with Eden's apple and the Devil. Why does water drown its lord? Why do so many minerals poison him? Why are so many plants and fishes deadly enemies? Why is the lord of creation subjected to the same laws of life as his subjects? Oh, all these things are satanic, or in some way connected with the first garden.

Now it never seems to occur to these far-seeing teachers that Nature's object in making animals and plants might possibly be first of all the happiness of each one of them, not the creation of all for the happiness of one. Why would man value himself as more than a small part of the one great unit of creation? And what creature of all that the Lord has taken the pains to make is not essential to the completeness of the unit – the cosmos? The universe would be incomplete without man, but it would also be incomplete without the smallest trans-microscopic creature that dwells beyond our conceitful eyes and knowledge."[159] In other words, the cosmos is interconnected, but not in the sense that we think of when we think of wi-fi and the internet and cyberspace. We are connected spiritually, and the only way you can get that sense of connectedness is in nature. In being alone and silent in the forests and streams and lakes and mountains and sea-shores that surround us.

We live in a society that has done its best to isolate us from nature. When we are isolated from nature, we are isolated from seeing reality. All the senses come alive when you are in the forests, or wading in a steam to fish for trout, or hiking along a trail in the mountains, or on a seashore taking in the vastness of the ocean surrounding you. When you are gazing at the two-dimensional screen on your 'smart phone,' you are not being aware of your surroundings. You are

---

[159] E. W. Teale, editor; *The Wilderness World of John Muir;* Houghton Mifflin Co.; 1982; pp. 316-317.

limiting your sense of reality to two dimensions, not three or four. You are losing touch with the real world around you and isolating yourself to the smaller world of the screen on your 'smart phone.'

"To be absorbed in the sheer otherness of any created order (nature) or beauty is to open the door to God, because it involves that basic displacement of the dominating ego without which there can be no spiritual growth."[160] When we view and sense the grandeur and vastness of the universe around us; the oceans and sky and acres of green forest, our self-centeredness begins to fall away. When we live in human constructed cities and spend all our time in them or in our human built homes, we are easily fooled by our self-absorption. We stagnate spiritually. We must get out into nature to experience the Holy Other.

I remember once I was in a restaurant waiting for a friend. Four men came in and sat down at a table in front of me. No words were spoken. All four men were busy looking at their 'smart phones.' Time went by and still no words were spoken between them, as I observed, for more than 10 minutes. My friend arrived and we began to talk. Still, as I observed, the four men continued on their 'smart phone.' If this is not devotion to technology, then I don't know what is. These four men were together, but not together. Rather than enjoying each other's company, they were enjoying the company of a life-less device that brings them only a small slice of reality, that they obviously have chosen to believe over the world around them.

As I think of this experience in a restaurant, I begin to understand how we are becoming a society where God is less and less, and we are more and more. How can we connect with an invisible God if we are constantly busy? If the first thing we see in the morning is our 'smart phone' screen and the last thing we see at night is our 'smart phone' screen, how does God get an opportunity to speak through the world of nature around us? It seems to me, we are sleepwalking into the future, through the wide gate of destruction, relying on our technology to save us from ourselves.

---

[160] Williams, R.; *Christian Spirituality*; John Knox Press; 1979; p. 176.

TEN SQUARED

10^2 is the math expression for 100. 10^1 is the math expression for 10. And 10^0 is the math expression for 1. These are called powers of ten. So, what? Well, they have a lot to do with three of Jesus' parables in the book of Luke, and furthermore they tell an amazing story about the grace and love of God for us and his creation.

Let's start with 100 – "Suppose one of you has a hundred sheep and loses one of them. Does not he leave the ninety-nine in the open country and go after the lost sheep until he finds it?"[161]

Next; 10 – "Or suppose a woman has ten silver coins and loses one. Does she not light a lamp, sweep the house and search carefully until she finds it?"[162]

Finally; 1 – The parable of the lost son, or the prodigal son. A famous story of a man who had two sons and one was lost and was found.[163]

Many things to notice in these three parables of Jesus:

- There is something lost and then found
- There is a party or celebration afterwards.
- There are animals, money and people involved in being lost.
- Two parables are short, and one is long
- Jesus' examples move through a sequence of powers of ten.

---

[161] Luke 15:4 NIV
[162] Luke 15:8 NIV
[163] Luke 15:11-31 NIV.

- All the parables have to do with welcoming 'sinners' and having a meal/celebration with them.
- None of these parables are very practical, or efficient in our modern way of thinking.

My first four observations about these parables are straight forward. They are some of the givens of the parables and I don't think anyone would argue over my first 4 observations. But then we run into some curious observations. Why does Jesus use a sequence of 100, then 10, then 1? What is that all about? My first way of thinking about this is the idea that the three parables get more and more personal. They move from one in a hundred out in the countryside and then one in ten in a house and then one of two in a very close family relationship: father and sons. In a way, Jesus is saying that we would search for our possessions (animals/money) diligently, and wait for our close relations to come back home. God is represented by the shepherd, the woman and the father in these three parables. God doesn't pursue us humans as in the parables of the sheep and the coin; God respects our freedom to search for Him as well. God is looking and waiting for us to return home. In short; God is our home. God is the 'ground of all being.'[164]

Then how do they all have to do with 'sinners' and having a meal/celebrating? Have you ever been to a party with not food? I haven't. There is usually food of some sort at a party. So, when you celebrate you usually eat. Eating is a sign of community. Having a meal together helps people bond together as a community. It involves a lot of sharing; a lot of talking. And Jesus in these three parables is saying that this eating and celebrating involves 'sinners.' The lost sheep, the lost coin, the lost son, are the 'sinners' that were lost and now are found. Celebrate!

And why are these examples of grace and lostness not practical or efficient? Well, if you lose one sheep out of ninety-nine, why would you risk the ninety-nine to go after just one? And if you lose

---

[164] First used by Paul Tillich, a 20th century theologian. See his work entitled "The New Being."

one coin, why would you spend so much time and effort looking for the one that is lost? And then why would you spend more money on celebrating when you found it? Why would you spend a lot of money on a son who squandered his inheritance? Why not just welcome him home and leave it at that? Wouldn't that help ease any tensions with his brother? So, what's the point, since these examples of lost/found are so impractical? In my way of thinking it is about the extravagance of God. And this is the 'hinge' for our thinking: God's resources are overwhelming when it comes to love and forgiveness: GRACE. "But where sin increased, grace increased all the more."[165]

"Oh, the overwhelming, never-ending, reckless love of God. Oh, it chases me down, fights 'til I'm found, leaves the ninety-nine. I couldn't earn it, and I don't deserve it, still, you give Yourself away. Oh, the overwhelming, never-ending, reckless love of God,"[166]

---

[165] Romans 5: 20b NIV
[166] Cory Asbury; chorus from "Reckless Love," 2017.

A MEAL TOGETHER

A meal: Fast food; foodies; prepared meals from 'on-line' sources; quick and efficient meals, healthy meals; lonely meals. Let's "eat and get on with our lives" meals. Let's go to church and have the shortest communion we can have service. Let's miss the meaning meals. Let's just get it over and done.

"After taking the cup, he gave thanks and said, "Take this and divide it among you. For I tell you I will not drink again of this fruit of the vine until the kingdom of God comes." And he took the bread, gave thanks and broke it. And gave it to them, saying, "This is my body given for you; do this in remembrance of me." In the same way, after supper he took the cup. Saying "This cup is the new covenant in my blood, which is poured out for you.""[167] Does this sound like a fast food meal to you? Did Jesus' disciples just eat and run to the garden of Gethsemane so Jesus could be arrested, and crucified? In the book of John, the gospel writer takes 5 chapters of his book to relate the conversation that happened during this Last Supper of Jesus. This was no fast food meal to get to the main point of the scriptures. This was no lonely meal hurriedly eaten before the big day. This was a communion; and I don't mean what we do in church when we take 'communion.'

What has happened to our meals together? How have we gone astray from the meaning of having a meal together- A communion together as we share our food and thoughts for the day? In my

---

[167] Luke 22: 17-20. NIV

community, we recently had a block party.[168] We are an over 55 years of age community. There are a lot of wrinkles and aches and pains represented in our community. But I noticed that as we ate together and sang together a lot of those daily aches and pains seemed to disappear. Some older men and women were dancing and singing like they did long ago, when they were young. As I watched this transformation, I wondered what was going on. And then it occurred to me that we had discovered what Jesus knew so long ago. We shared a common meal and a common song. "When they had sung a hymn, they went out to the Mount of Olives."[169] At the base of The Mount of Olives there was the garden of Gethsemane. Most of us followers of Jesus know what that is. Notice that the disciples and Jesus did just what we did at our block party: ate and sang.

Meals and singing are the founding act of the Church of Jesus Christ; however, you want to define it. We call the meal the Eucharist, which means "thanksgiving" in Greek. We wrapped the Eucharist in ritual and meaning, even reserving it for members of our own congregations of worshippers: A kind of exclusionary form of Christianity.

If you read the Bible thoroughly you will find meal after meal after meal, served in all kinds of occasions. The Bible has a lot of meals being prepared, served and eaten. These meals include angels, prophets, sinners and saints. They don't distinguish who gets served and who doesn't. All that are present come to the table in the Bible. No one asks if they are Jewish or not, or if they are of the right sect or not; or if they have been baptized or not. In the Bible stories the people in the story are welcome at the table for a meal. In fact, one of the scandalous stories in the New Testament was about Jesus eating a meal with one of the Pharisees and an uninvited woman came in and slipped up behind Jesus and began washing his feet with her tears.[170]

---

[168] When a community blocks off a street and usually has a meal together. Everyone in the community contributes to the meal in some way.

[169] Mark 14: 26. NIV

[170] Luke 7: 36- 39. NIV

Did Jesus kick her out? Did he say that she did not belong there? Of course not. And that is what meals together are all about: together.

In the 14th chapter of the book of Luke there are a series of parables (metaphors) and examples that Jesus provides to get across the idea of what should be our priorities in life. The next chapter in Luke (15) is all about lost things. The overriding priority that Jesus talks about in Luke 14 is knowing your place in the universe. Knowing your place at a banquet, in a family, or planning your life. In all these priorities in your life you are humble. It is your humility that determines how you respond to banquets, your family, or your life plans. You number yourself among the least, and the lost. You know if you have the resources to plan the next part of your life. Read Luke 14 carefully and you understand why Jesus says at the end: "Are you listening to this? Really listening?"[171] Chapter 15 goes on to explain the meaning of the lost ones in this world.

Just so you don't get confused: we are all the lost ones in the world. That is why God is continually seeking us. That is why when we come together at the table, the common table of grace and eat together, that we begin to 'see' each other for real. Eating together is community building. Eating together is where we practice our humility, so we know Who is the priority in our lives.

"Our continuing witness to and fear-of-the-Lord participation in the work of salvation is formed eucharistically (the Last Supper) around our kitchen tables. Daily meals with family, friends, guests, acts of hospitality everyone, are the most natural and frequent settings for working out the personal and social implications of salvation."[172] What Peterson is saying here is a hinge to our understanding of what it means to be a follower of Jesus. Our community block party was a form of thanksgiving that we all participated in and shared a common bond during a meal and a song. The block party was rejuvenating. The meal and the song were acts of salvation; bringing us together in community.

---

171 Luke 14: 34b; *MSG*

172 E. Peterson; *Christ Plays in Ten Thousand Places;* Eerdman's Publishing Co.; 2005; p. 214.

That is what salvation is about: including all people at the table, eating meals together, singing songs together. Salvation is the process of realizing that we all in the same family; the family of God; the Kingdom of Heaven; "Thy Kingdom come."

PAGANS

There was a motorcycle group when I was young called The Pagans. They began in 1958 close to where I lived in Prince George's county Maryland. They even had a constitution and a president who was paid as much as the president of The United States. In today's dollars that would be over one million dollars. Quite a salary for a motorcycle gang president. They became known as an 'outlaw' motorcycle gang and attracted many returning soldiers from the Viet Nam war, who were looking for a way to continue the bonding of brothers they had experienced during the war. The ranks of The Pagans swelled in the 1960's and they had 'turf wars' with other motorcycle clubs like 'The Outlaws'or 'Bandidos.' The Pagans rode either British made Triumph motorcycles or Harley Davidson motorcycle. Since the 1970's The Pagans only ride Harley Davidson motorcycles and they have to be of a certain size. Since the 1990' to today (2019) members of The Pagans have been involved in numerous criminal activities including small street drug trafficking, assault, arson, extortion, motorcycle/car theft, and weapons trafficking. Most of the violence carried out by the Pagans is directed to rival gangs such as the HAMC[173].

So why am I talking about motorcycle gangs. Well, it's the name. The Pagans. What is a pagan and how does this relate to Christianity? The term 'pagan' originally meant 'rural' in Latin, but over the years as with a lot of other terms it has changed considerably. Now, when you think of the word 'pagan' you probably think of a person who believes in a whole range of 'religions' from polytheism to witches

---

[173] Hell's Angels Motorcycle Club

and the New Age movement in America. There are a whole lot of other 'isms' with many different beliefs attached to them. What I think modern 'pagans' have in common is a way of thinking that involves some form of magic, rituals, and a need for personal power of some sort. I think these are people who basically feel powerless in this world. And this is not an uncommon feeling for most of us humans. When faced with the political and social events going on around us, we all feel powerless to do anything about them. So, we need some way to feel that we have some 'power' of some sort to come to our aid when the world around us goes so terribly wrong. We long for our enemies to get their 'just rewards.'[174] We long for this thing we call 'justice.'

And how we think about 'justice' is an important 'hinge' in our understanding as Christians to be in this world, but not of this world that we live in. What is 'justice?' I am going to begin with a Bible verse: "God made him who had no sin to be sin for us, so that we might become the righteousness of God."[175] Boy, Paul says a lot with few words! I think the word 'righteousness' in this verse is what gets us all confused. What I think Paul is saying is that us Christians are the 'righteousness of God' because we have been freed from sin through the cross of Jesus and therefore, we are 'justified.' And there again is that term 'justice' in the form of 'justified.' Since we Christians have been 'justified' through Christ, then Christ *is* our justice. Confused? Let me put it another way: Jesus wasn't the victim of God's justice (as some Christians claim) but he embodied God's 'justice.' When we conclude that Jesus was the victim of God's justice we are thinking like a 'pagan.' If Jesus satisfied the demands of a wrathful god, then he was just a sacrificial lamb on the altar of the 'justice' of God. And that is what 'pagans' do in some form or another. If you look at the modern 'pagan' religions, they have rituals that involve some kind of sacrifice to achieve their forms of 'justice.' Their enemies getting their 'just rewards.'

There are many Christian songs that have lyrics that refer to

---

[174] The punishment that someone deserves.
[175] 2 Corinthians 5:21. NIV

this wrathful concept of God demanding the sacrifice of his only begotten son, Jesus. 1) "Who you say I am:" lyric – 'free at last he ransomed me.[176] 2) "Reckless Love:" lyric – 'you paid it all for me.[177] 3) "Come to The Altar:" lyric- 'forgiveness was bought with the precious blood of Jesus Christ.[178] 4) "O Love Divine what Hast Thou Done:" lyric- 'ye all are bought with Jesus blood.[179] 5) "There is a Fountain Filled with Blood:" lyric –'til all the ransomed church of God be saved, to sin no more.[180] And I could go on, but I think you get the point. This ransom idea for Jesus' crucifixion has been with us a long time. In my mind this is a 'pagan' way to think about the crucifixion's purpose. This is the same as Jesus taking the place of us sinners getting our 'just rewards' to satisfy the 'wrath of God.'

Jesus is our 'justice,' just as Jesus is the Christ. Just as Jesus is the King of Kings and Lord of Lords. "He is the image of the invisible God, the firstborn over **all** creation. For by him **all** things were created: things in heaven and on earth, visible and invisible, whether thrones or powers or rulers or authorities; **all** things were created by him and for him."[181] It makes sense then, if ALL things visible and invisible were created by him and for him, then Jesus the Christ would be 'justice.' That is just one of His attributes.

And then when we use terms such as 'social justice' or 'restoring justice,' we miss the point. What kind of 'justice' would not be social? What kind of 'justice' would not be restoring things to their 'self-evident truths' or 'inalienable rights'? So, then to put 'justice' in the realm of a 'pagan' way of thinking just comes up short. When we separate 'justice' from Jesus the Christ we are thinking like 'pagans.'

"Take a good look at my servant. I'm backing him to the hilt. He's the one I chose, and I couldn't be more pleased with him. I've bathed him with my Spirit, my life. He'll set everything right among

---

[176] R. Morgan & B. Fielding; Hillsong Worship sheet music; 2018
[177] C. Asbury, C. Culver & R. Jackson; Bethel Music; 2017
[178] C. Brown, M. Brock, S. Furtick & W. Joy; Elevation Worship; 2017
[179] C. Wesley; 1742. This hymn has been published in 136 hymnals.
[180] W. Cowper; 1772. This hymn has been published in 2189 hymnals.
[181] Colossians 1:15 – 16. NIV; bold type mine.

the nations (**justice**). He won't call attention to what he does with loud speeches or gaudy parades. He won't brush aside the bruised and the hurt and he won't disregard the small and insignificant, but he'll steadily and firmly set things right (**justice**). He won't tire out and quit. He won't be stopped until he's finished his work -setting things right on earth (**justice**)."[182] Who is our Justice? Who is the Lord and Law of life?

---

[182] Isaiah 42: 1- 4a; *MSG*. Parenthesis and bold type mine.

ABANDONMENT[183]

Many wise women and men have said that our greatest fear in life is abandonment. Left alone. Feelings of total unworthiness. Being mocked and made nothing in the eyes of others. Totally alone; abandoned.

This is what happened to Jesus before his crucifixion. And not only was he abandoned and completely alone, he was mocked, tortured and finally killed in his com-plete abandonment. He was the 'desolating sacrilege' that Daniel foretold many years before Him. In the crucifixion we see the raw power of God. The real power of the universe. God refuses to let us go. God refuses to let us be abandoned. God willingly sacrifices his Son so that we won't be alone and abandoned. Over and over Jesus told us of the lost things redeemed; the lost coin, the lost sheep, the lost son. All those parables tell us that God will not abandon us. God will die to keep us. God will cause his only Son to die, to show His eternal love for us.

And even worse, we all killed his only Son. We all shouted, "crucify him!" Not just once, but over and over, because we refused and refuse to "see" who He really is: The King of the Universe. You may ask: "When did I do this?" My answer is when you choose your wants, needs and desires over someone else. When you worship your holy trinity and not God's. When you bow down to the idols of this age. When you ignore and refuse to hear God calling you in the business of your life. We all shout, "crucify him!" We are sinners,

---

[183] To desert, to leave alone, adrift, non-support.

and if you don't 'get' it, you don't know yourself. You are lost in the pride and arrogance of this world.

God is revealed when He seems the most hidden. Who could "see" God in this abandonment of Jesus on the cross? Even Jesus cries out "My God, my God, why have you forsaken me.?"[184] It was his abandonment that was too much for him to bear. Even God the Father turned his back on Him. If you allow yourself to begin to feel His complete abandonment, you will begin to understand the sorrow of Christ Jesus. Yet Jesus was willing to allow this to happen to Him for my sake. The One who knew The Father and The Spirit for all time, suffered this cross, this abandonment. "He took the punishment, that made us whole. Through His bruises we get healed."[185]

The Church of Jesus Christ has confused and misled many people on what the crucifixion was about. Sometimes making out that God is a wrathful bean counter, needing some sacrifice to balance the scales of justice that we sinners have so long ignored and trampled on. That in some way God needs to be 'justified' for all our sins. We are not realizing that God does not need any justification; God is God alone. God alone is good. Read what Jesus said about God. "And Jesus said to him: "Why do you call me good? There is none good but one, God.""[186] So, then, how can this Good God demand a penalty for our sin? Is God miserly with love for us? Certainly not.

Was God miserly as he spent billions of years perfecting the cells that make us up? Was God miserly when He created a sun that would shine for billions of years to allow the evolution of conscious beings on this planet? Was God miserly when He laid down the laws of the universe that favored living things? Was God miserly when He caused the many singularities that produced permanence in the myriad biological functions that keep us alive each day? Isn't it more of a miracle that you function as well as you do, day after day, then when you get sick and diseased and you have a miraculous cure?

---

[184] Matthew 27:43 NIV
[185] Isaiah 53:5 *MSG.*
[186] Mark 10:18 NIV.

Dying is the way of the universe and life. We are all going to die, but God has chosen to lavish his love on us in ways that we do not comprehend. We are too busy being busy. No! God is a good Father. God is a good Mother. And God abandoned His only Son to show His love for us.

It is in this extreme loneliness of Jesus that I enter a universe of extreme poverty of being, of sheer silence in His presence, in the void and emptiness of my personal meaning. It is here I begin an understanding of the cross "towering over the wrecks of time."[187] It is at the 'foot of the cross' that the richness and life-giving fountain of creation is given its full meaning. The cross is exactly that: the meeting point of visible and invisible, the physical display of God's glory and grace, where God shows us who He/She truly is. At the cross there are no signs of transcendence; there is only suffering and love. It is in this extreme abandonment of Jesus the Christ where we can lay down all our burdens of thought and circumstance and worship in awe and reverence. God is simply God.

"The Word is rejected and crucified by the world; only when we see that there is no place for the Word in the world do, we see that he is God's **Word**, the Word of the hidden, transcendent creator. And *then, only then*, can we see, hear, experience (if you will) the newness of that creative God, resurrection and grace, new life out the ultimate negation and despair."[188] This is why there is so much emphasis of emptying yourself in Christian thought. It is when you are ready to let go of yourself enough to let the hidden Word speak to you at the cross of Christ Jesus. It is when you realize that you have rejected the very Word that created the universe and condemned Christ to die on a cross, that you can see for real the hidden Otherness of God. This is where you see the indescribable, incomparable, nonsensical, love of God.

---

[187] "In The Cross of Christ I Glory;" John Bowring; 1825. "wrecks of time" is a reference to all the governments, kingdoms, and political countries throughout time.

[188] Williams, R.; *Christian Spirituality*; John Knox Press; 1979; p. 178.

DIASPORA

Now here is a word you don't see too often. Diaspora: has come to refer to involuntary mass dispersions of a population from its original territory. In other words when a group of people are dispersed out of their homeland to other parts of the world. And the word homeland means where a people 'originally' were from. And as Followers of Jesus we have been dispersed throughout the world from our homeland: The Kingdom of God. We are a diaspora. And I think that is the way we need to be as The Kingdom of God.

Some American Christians get very upset with this idea that we are a diaspora. American Christians like to think that America is a "Christian Nation." But we are not a Christian nation and haven't been since our inception as a nation. If you look up the 'religions' of many of our "founding fathers", you will find they were deists or at best 'lukewarm' Christians. This is not a way to discredit them, but to say they were people of their time: The Age of Enlightenment.

Christianity is in decline in America and will continue to be in decline[189]. More and more Americans no longer see a need for being associated with a church or for their children to be brought up in a faith of any kind. America still has the greatest number of practicing Christians than any other country in the world, most of them being Protestants.

So then, as time moves on, America will be less and less Christian and more and more 'secular.'[190] And this is what I mean when I say we

---

[189] See Pewforum.org for more details.

[190] attitudes, activities, or other things that have no religious or spiritual basis.

are a diaspora. As with other parts of the world, we followers of Jesus will be a smaller part of the population of a nation than the country we call our homeland. If you look at where Christianity is present throughout the world you will find we have populations of Christians in virtually every country in the world.[191] That hasn't always been true. We certainly didn't start out that way.

To be a diaspora or a smaller part of a population is not a bad thing in my mind. This gives us a way to be 'in the world but not of the world.' As a diaspora we can be a "city on a hill" and be the "salt of the earth."[192] The imagery I get is like salt, we are sprinkled on the earth, and like seeds we are sown on the earth, whether the ground we are sown in is rocky, or has thorns, or is good soil for growth. We are there, in the countries of the world to be a light and flavor to the world; sometimes we grow and sometimes we don't, depending on the country we find ourselves in, but still we are there as a witness to the Way of Jesus the Christ.

"Too often concerns for the status of the church tempts some to employ desperate measures to ensure that the church will remain socially significant or at least have a majority of the population. But the church is not called to be significant or large. The church is called to be apostolic. Faithfulness, not numbers or status, should be the characteristic that shapes the witness of the church."[193] It may be that God is causing our numbers to decrease in America, so that we, like the disciples will learn to travel light.[194]

After all, it is going to take a lot more time for the world to get the message of the Way of Jesus the Christ. The people of the world have a lot of 'globalization' to do. There is a lot more mixing of the world's populations and communication systems and distribution of goods systems to go through before the world is ready for membership into the Kingdom of God. But the way I see it we are there, throughout the world, ready to serve, ready to suffer for the Kingdom of God.

[191] See en.wikipedia.org/wiki/Christiantyby country#By country
[192] Matthew 5:13 & 14. NIV
[193] S. Hauerwas; *Matthew*, Brazos Press; 2015; p.107.
[194] see Matthew 10:9-10. NIV

Are you ready for a worldwide vision for Christianity? Are you ready for an enlargement of your view of who this Jesus is? Well, maybe it's time you re-read the book of Colossians.

"He was supreme in the beginning and – leading the resurrection parade – he is supreme in the end. From beginning to end he is there, towering far above everything, absolutely everything, **everyone**. So spacious is he, so roomy, that everything of God finds its proper place in him without crowding. Not only that, but all the broken and dislocated pieces of the universe – **people** and things, animals and atoms -get **properly fixed together** in vibrant harmonies, all because of his death, his blood poured down from the Cross."[195] I have bold-typed the words as they relate to my idea of the diaspora of us Christians in the world. It is going to take a long time for us **people of the world to get properly fixed together so everyone who is broken and dislocated can become the Kingdom of God on Earth: "Thy Kingdom Come. Thy will be done, on earth as it is in heaven."**[196]

And again, this is why the Cross of Jesus is the central piece of the puzzle for us humans on planet earth. It is through this sacrifice that we are brought together as one family of God. This is the one physical act in the universe that brings it all together for the New Creation. And in that final day we will 'see' a "New heaven and a new earth for the first heaven and the first earth had passed away, and there was no longer any sea. I saw the Holy City, the new Jerusalem coming down out of heaven from God, prepared as a bride beautifully dressed for her husband. And I heard a loud voice from the throne saying, "Now the dwelling of God is with men, and he will live with them. They will be his people, and God himself will be with them and be their God.""[197] There is a lot of imagery here in these verses from the book of Revelation, so don't get caught up in the imagery. Hear the central message: All things will be made new and God will live with us. God

---

[195] Colossians 1:18-20. *MSG.*
[196] I think we know where this is from.
[197] Revelation 21:1-3. NIV.

won't just dwell in a tabernacle in the desert of Israel, God will be present in the world: Emmanuel.

The guessing game of whether there is a God or not will come to an end. And this Scripture will come true: "Then the end will come, when he hands over the kingdom to God the Father after he has destroyed all dominion, authority and power. For he must reign until he has put all his enemies under his feet. The last enemy to be destroyed is death. For he "Has put everything under his feet""[198] When Paul talks about destroying all 'dominion, authority and power' he is talking about the governments of this world. The metaphor of 'putting all his enemies under his feet' is put another way by saying that all Christ's enemies will be loved, so that they too will worship Him as us followers of Jesus do now.

---

[198] 1 Corinthians 15: 24-27a NIV.

WAR

I have saved this 'hinge' in thinking until last. This is probably the most controversial 'hinge' that I have to offer. You may consider me to be a 'turncoat' or unpatriotic when you read this 'hinge' in my thinking. I hope you don't see it that way. I see patriotism as a love for country that is in the right perspective: when we see our country as a great country among many other great countries in the world. Each country in the world is great because of the unique people that make it up. It is great because we are all in the same family of God. We are all born as a member of the image of God. I believe in a world form of patriotism. Or as the song goes: "This is my song, O God of all the nations, a song of peace for lands afar and mine. This is my home, the country where my heart is; here are my hopes, my dreams, my holy shrine. But, other hearts in other lands are beating, with hopes and dreams as true and high as mine."[199]

I have often wondered about my friends who were fascinated and almost enthralled by the Civil War in America. I did not share their enthusiasm to know all the details and study the battlefields and stroll through the historical monuments that encompassed my state of Maryland. And then there were the pilgrimages to Gettysburg that my friends took to study the great battle that was the turning point for The Civil War, allowing The North to win and The South to lose. I kept wondering why this war was so important to them. I wondered why this war had a religious aura to it. I wondered why this war has so much attention given to it, when it was the first war that Americans

---

[199] G. Harkness, L. Stone; "A Hymn of Peace;" 1934.

115

were the only combatants and the only victims at the same time, or as they often said, "brother fought against brother." The Civil War was the deadlist war in American history if you consider not just the soldiers, but the total number of Americans who lost their lives because of this war.[200] That total number exceeds any other war in which we have been engaged by over 200,000 deaths! So, the Civil War exacted a great sacrifice for the American people.

I want to concentrate on this 'sacrifice' of American people as a starting point in my understanding of why this Civil War is so revered in America. Let me start with a quote from one of the Senators in congress at the time:

"But, fellow citizens, the war which we wage is not merely for ourselves; it is for all mankind...In ending slavery here we open its gates all over the world, and let the oppressed go free. Nor is this all. In saving the republic we shall save civilization.... In such a cause no effort can be too great, no faith can be too determined. To die for country is pleasant and honorable. **But all who die for country now die for humanity. Wherever they lie, in killing fields, they will be remembered as the heroes through whom the republic was saved, and civilization established forever.**"[201]

I have bold typed the last two sentences in this quote to highlight what was happening in America at the time. The Civil War was being elevated to a level of 'sacrifice' that rivaled Jesus the Christ. And like the Christ they will be remembered because of their 'blood sacrifice.' There is a last supper feel to these times, that America needed to remember over and over the sacrifices that were made for not just America, but for the world. There was a massive sacrifice being made on the nations 'altar' that was represented by the American flag. It was only after the Civil War that Americans displayed 'the flag' on buildings to show support for 'the troops.' Before this war 'the flag'

---

[200] Just Goggle: United States military casualties of war.

[201] Charles Sumner; abolitionist senator from Massachusetts; in office from 1851-1874. You might want to look up "The caning of Charles Sumner" for further insights.

was rarely found but on ships to designate that the ship was from America and of course military forts, like Fort McHenry.[202]

Sounds like a parallel to John 3:16 to me, only if we changed it to reference the American Civil War it would read: 'America so loved the world that she gave her sons, that whoever believes in America will not die, but have eternal life.' So, in a very important sense the sacrifices of the Civil War became a religion in America. And honoring the dead now became equivalent to a belief in a kind of god: The Honored Dead. And we have trouble separating the past from the future in this regard. President Lincoln said in the Gettysburg Address: "that from these honored dead we take increased devotion to that cause for which they gave the last full measure of devotion— that we here highly resolve that these dead shall not have died in vain..." If I may unpack this famous quote a little. What does it mean to say that these 'honored dead' did not die in vain? Does this mean that when we send our sons and daughters out to war that they continue the sacrifices for our country so that the soldiers of the past "did not die in vain?" Does this idea set up a culture that shows that its link to the past is a heritage that creates more and more soldiers who **do not** "die in vain?" And then does this 'military culture' in America then become separated from the general ethics of the American society?

It is very difficult to **not** honor the people who gave their lives for our country. America made an attempt at this idea after the Viet Nam war. Soldiers who came home were treated very 'dishonorably' by many Americans, who had been lied to by our government about the Viet Nam war and took out their anger on the returning soldiers, creating a lot of division in America. Honoring our dead soldiers is an important value to have as a nation. They need to be remembered and honored, but for the right reasons. They need to remembered to help us understand that war is evil, and we need to prevent it. That we need to remember their sacrifices to help us **not** repeat them, over and over as we have continued to do since the Civil War.

---

[202] This is where, during the war of 1812, that Francis S. Key wrote the "Star Spangled Banner," our national anthem.

"What's past is prologue." In our modern use, this phrase stands for the idea that history sets the context for the present. The quotation is engraved on the National Archives Building in Washington, DC. It was first used by Shakespeare in his play The Tempest. It is commonly used by the military when discussing the similarities between wars throughout history. The phrase helps give us the sense that war is just a part of who we are. It is the way things have been and the way things will be in the future. In my way of thinking this is pretty despairing.

It is very difficult to let go of the past and embrace the future. We live in the now, and not in the past or future. We need to learn the lessons from the past in order to embrace the future with hope and not despair. When we elevate our dead war heroes to the status of 'saviors' we are helping to continue the downward spiral of war. Our war heroes need to be honored and remembered but not elevated to a 'religion' of some sort. That only continues to make war a way of life, just like being a Christian is a way of life. If war is a way of life in America, then our government becomes like a god. It manages our security and our welfare. It provides the food and health care and whatever other 'rights' you can think of. In effect, our government becomes a god. And then you have two gods in America: our government and our God (the real one, YHWH/I AM).

Perspective is very difficult and needs to be practiced. To put our country in perspective with our God is very important. Every country needs a government of some sort, but that government must not be elevated to the status of a god. And that is where perspective comes in. I am amazed and continuously puzzled by how engrained violence and war are woven into our American culture. Let me start with a couple of quotes to give us some perspective:

"Warfare is almost as old as man himself, and reaches into the most secret places of the human heart, places where self-dissolves rational purpose, where pride reigns, where emotion is paramount, where instinct is king."[203] And another quote: "War is like a disease

---

[203] J. Keegan, *A History of Warfare;* Vintage Press, New York, 1993; p. 3.

that exhibits a capacity to mutate and mutates fastest in the face of efforts to control and eliminate it."[204]

Let me put these two quotes together to make more sense out of them. In the first quote I realize that the concept of war is a raw emotional element based on pride and I would add fear. And war is like a mutating disease that uses our good friend rationalization (the action of attempting to explain or justify behavior or an attitude with logical reasons, even if these reasons are not appropriate) to continue its long life in our world. As time as gone on, we have become better and better at 'rationalizing' our need for war.

Adding to this mix of honoring the dead soldiers and perspective is the brotherhood of soldiers. I have never been in war and I am lucky to have not been drafted in the Viet Nam war when I was young. And I thank all my friends and relatives for going to Viet Nam and doing what they thought was right for our country. They are truly loyal Americans and need to be honored and respected for their service to America. And there is a brotherhood that forms with soldiers and other combatants that I will not be a part of, because I did not 'go to war.' Let me use a couple of quotes to illustrate my point:

"Those men on the line (battlefield) were my family, my home. They were closer to me than I can say, closer than any friends had been or would be. They never let me down. And I couldn't do it to them. I had to be with them, rather than let them die and me live with the knowledge that I might have saved them. Men, I now know, do not fight for flag or country, for the Marine Corps or glory or any other abstraction. They fight for one another."[205] And another: "In military writings on unit cohesion (platoons, companies, etc.), one consistently finds the assertion that the bonds that combat soldiers

---

[204] S. Hauerwas, War and The American Difference; Baker Publishing Group, Grand Rapids Michigan; 2011; p.43.

[205] Quote from W. Manchester in Lt. Col. D. Grossman's book On Killing: The Psychological Cost of Learning to Kill in War and Society; Boston; Little, Brown; 1995; p. 2.

form with one another are stronger than the bonds most men have with their wives."[206]

Both of these quotes are about the bond that men in combat form with each other. This bond between men in war creates a brotherhood that those of us outside of combat don't know or understand. And we need to find a way to bring these bonded brothers back into our American culture, which all too often abandons them and treats them very poorly. These bonded brothers need to be told that they did what was 'right' for our country. They need to get medals. They need to be loved and cared for by other Americans who do not know what they went through. And they need to be forgiven.

And this need to be forgiven brings me to another perspective about war: When we send people to fight a war, we ask them for a great sacrifice if they survive- the sacrifice of their unwillingness to kill. Did you get that? These warriors must do something they have been taught all their lives not to do: You shall not kill. And that is a sacrifice that puts them in great moral pain. There is story after story of soldiers who returned from war (the survivors) and lived with the horror of what they did to other human beings. They spend years and years learning to forgive themselves.[207]

I had relatives by birth and marriage that were in World War II. My father in law was part of a second wave of soldiers to land on the beach at Normandy during that war. My wife's uncle was a tail gunner on a navy war plane in the Pacific Ocean. Neither one of them talked about their war experiences until they were old men. They kept it all to themselves for many years. Whether they shared their war experiences with their wives, I will never know. But, fortunately for me, they shared with me what they did during the war, before they died. An important point with both these men is that they were in combat, but did not kill any enemy soldiers face to face. They did not know the bond of brotherhood that so many

---

[206] Ibid., p.149.

[207] If you want to read some of these stories get a copy of D. Grossman's book; *On Killing: The Psychological Cost of Learning to Kill in War and Society*; Boston; Little, Brown; 1995.

soldiers knew because they had killed the enemy face to face. They had not sacrificed their unwillingness to kill. And I think that is why they were able to return to 'normality' better than the soldiers who had sacrificed their unwillingness to kill.

And then we get this idea of 'terrorism' all confused. We link 'terrorism' to war and even have a Global War on Terrorism, started after the attack on the World Trade Center on September 11, 2001. Now we have a global war sanctioned by many countries, and that certainly contributes to our mutating disease called war. And then we have all forms of terrorism occurring both outside and within of our borders; called 'home grown[208]' or otherwise. Did you know there are over 100 definitions of terrorism? What a quagmire we have. Confusion reigns supreme as it does in war. To add a little perspective: Our colonists who faced the British troops in Boston, Massachusetts were considered terrorists[209] by many loyalists to the British government and some in the British parliament. It was all a matter of perspective.

But none of these lessons in perspective gets to the real problem facing the world and its need for war. "And lead us not into temptation, but deliver us from the evil one."[210] Most of us know some variation of this part of the Lord's Prayer. But, lets focus on the link between leading us not into temptation and delivering us from evil part. We are led into temptation when we consider the need for war. We are led into temptation when we want to kill all the terrorists in the world. We are led into temptation when we separate the killing in war from crime and acts of passion, when we believe that war is an exception to the commandment: Thou shall not kill. These temptations can only NOT deliver us from evil. Pure and simple: war is evil, and we need to begin a way to end it.

Before I get too far from the topic, I want to clarify the difference

---

[208] If you want an exercise in futility, look up domestic terrorism on the internet.

[209] If you want to see how look up 'The Sons of Liberty' before and during the American Revolution.

[210] The Lord's Prayer; Matthew 6:13 NIV

between policing and warfare. I will start with a quote from John Yoder: "It is structural and a profound difference in the sociological meaning of the appeal of force[211]. In the police function, the violence or threat thereof is applied only to the offending party. The use of violence by the agent of the police is subject to review by higher authorities. The police officer applies power **within the limits of a state** whose legislation even the criminal knows are applicable to him. In any orderly police system, there are serious **safeguards** to keep the violence of the police from being applied in a wholesale way against the innocent. The police power **generally is great enough to overwhelm** that of the individual offender so that any resistance on the offender's part is pointless. In all of these aspects war is structurally different. The doctrine of a "just war" is an effort to extend into the realm of war the logic of the limited violence of police authority – but not a very successful one."[212] [bold type and underline mine]

Yes, there is a big difference between war and policing[213]. The main point to me is that there are 'limits' and 'safeguards' to keep the necessary violence of police from getting innocent people caught up in the processes of policing. Unfortunately, we live in a society that needs policing. There are a lot of people who do not obey the laws and don't wish to.

We need police to be an intimidating presence. This is part of the force that is needed that is 'great enough to overwhelm' offenders. When we ask police to be as polite and politically correct as they can, we are asking them not to be deterrents to crime. For me, it is a good thing that I fear the police, but I am not afraid of them. They keep by worse self in check. And if there are any of us 'out there' who think

---

[211] This 'appeal to force' is a logical fallacy. It is best summed by the statement: "If you don't do X, then I will hurt you." Or as we have heard many times from bullies: "Or else."

[212] J. H. Yoder; *The Politics of Jesus*; Eerdmans Publishing Co.; 1994; p. 234

[213] Wars generally have few rules other than kill the enemy by whatever means necessary. Yes, we have the 'Geneva Conventions,' but they are too often broken by both sides of any war. There are numerous examples.

we don't have a 'worse self,' then they need to find a good counselor and find their darker side.

We need the police to be well trained, not only in the laws, but in handling situations that can produce some really horrific results. I need only mention the recent media frenzies over police mistakes, due to lack of good training.

We need to ensure that our police officers are mentally stable and calm in the face of their own personal safety and the safety of citizens that they protect. Again, good training is the answer. When we hire ex-military people to the police force that have been trained in the 'art of war,' we need to make sure that they know the difference between policing and war. I am not sure that that issue is even addressed in police officer training- But I am sure it is needed.

We need the world to 'catch up' to the 'Christian' way of doing things. A non-violent way as exemplified in the Sermon on The Mount. And here is another perspective that us followers of Jesus need to live: What is it that is worth dying for rather than what is worth killing for? This is the Christian perspective. This is the non-violent perspective. We live in an American culture that asks us to kill for our country if and when we go to war. This is contrary to our faith in Jesus the Christ. And the alternative to war for followers of Jesus is worship. So then, the Church of Jesus Christ is an alternative to war: it **is** an ethical position of faith.

That is why us "Christians" need to be a people separate from the world; in the world but not of the world. We need to keep alive the hope and vision of a day when wars will cease.

"Keep bright in us the vision of a day when war shall cease, when hatred and division give way to love and peace, till dawns the morning glorious when truth and justice reign, and Christ shall rule victorious o'er all the worlds' domain."[214]

---

[214] "O God of Every Nation;" *The United Methodist Hymnal;* United Methodist Publishing House; Nashville Tenn.; 1989; p. 435.

Printed in the United States
By Bookmasters